The Christian Tragic Hero

The Christian Tragic Hero In French and English Literature

George Ross Ridge
Professor

and

Benedict Chiaka Njoku
Distinguished Professor

HUMANITIES PRESS INC.
Atlantic Highlands, NJ

Copyright© 1983 by Humanities Press Inc.

First published in 1983 in the United States of America by Humanities Press Inc.,
Atlantic Highlands, NJ 07716

Library of Congress Cataloging in Publication Data

Ridge, George Ross.
  The Christian tragic hero in French and English literature.

  Bibliography: p.
  Includes index.
  1. French literature--History and criticism.   2. English literature--History
and criticism.   3. Heroes in literature.   4. Christianity in literature.
5. Tragic, The.   I. Njoku, Benedict Chiaka.   II. Title.
PQ145.1.H4R52   1983   820'.9'352   83-4297
ISBN 0-391-02858-8

Manufactured in the United States of America

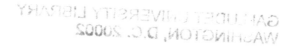

A Table of Contents

A Dedication

This work is dedicated to great humanists who believe in quality humanistic education for all people and to Mrs. Josephine Njoku for her zeal for self-improvement.

Acknowledgments

Thanks are due to the staff of Leontyne Price Library and the staff of The University of Mississippi Library for help in locating research materials, to the National Endowment for the Humanities for reading the manuscript and providing helpful advice and criticism, and to all those who provided encouragement when the manuscript was in preparation.

Préface et Dénouement:
Ave atque Vale

These essays will startle you, even if you are a professor—particularly if you are a professor. In the America that values (and, alas, overvalues) analysis, they represent synthesis: impressions. Moreover, as synthesis, they are highly impressionistic and quite heretical, as if they had stepped full blown from Walter Pater's *Studies in the Renaissance* in the perfumed Oxford don's satin-pillow-lined office late in the British *décadence,* among the blue vases with lilacs and cornflowers and, above all, beside the cocaine syringe.

We make no apologies for our essays. Of course, we are sophisticated enough to realize that few of you will concur with much of what we say. And if we are appreciated at all, it will doubtlessly be in a far more sympathetic Europe and throughout the Third World, since we are Third Worlders ourselves, and not in an America obsessed with the overly cerebral analyses of its disquieting and never very illuminating *explications de texte.* For, in a word, we are, as avowedly Catholic critics in the rich and sometimes lush heritage of our peculiar and particular Christian Communion, catalysts: catalysts. We do not ask you to accept our judgments. We ask you only to respond, either for or against our *impressions,* themselves often *heretical impressions,* and, if you will, respond in print to our pointed but never pontifical points of view.

This alone is our critical success in the life of academia, as Professor Pater might say: to elicit your response: your *impression.* Publish your impressions of our solipsistic points of view, if you will, if you insist, if you must; for we couldn't keep quiet ourselves. Or, better yet, think along with us and recount your impressions to your students or among yourselves, as you wax poetic, and perhaps verbose, and even grandiloquent, in the miasma of the martini seas of your *faisandé* faculty cocktail parties.

Who knows?

Perhaps there are too many academic books already: or, as Mallarmé might write, "hélas, j'ai lu tous les livres!"

Indeed, who can tell?

But this fact we guarantee. Our little book will not bore you—alarm you, perhaps, yes—but not weary you with curious and quaint overwrought details, with sundry footnotes—some of them headily manufactured, for we have known scholars who invented their own footnotes. As impressionistic critics, we want nothing more than this: just this. For our mission is to entertain you as well as to enlighten you, surely a classical goal worthy of Horace, surely a goal too that few self-respecting American professors would deem proper, fitting: "scholarly": "sufficiently academic."

We do not mind your objections. Object if you must. But give us an audience to a point of view *démodé* and *déclassé* since the Gay Nineties in London and Paris, when even the gold-headed canes of the syphilitic dandies and boulevardiers seemed curiously out of joint in time and space with the passing of the Second Empire and the puritanical ban on the bistro sale of absinthe.

Charlemagne as Christian Tragic Hero

It is singular that in *La Chanson de Roland* the great King Charlemagne should be so often alluded to and so rarely make his appearance. Or is it so remarkable, indeed, or rather the very clever artifice of a most gifted epic poet? As a matter of fact, Homer does something very similar in the greatest of all the Occidental epics, *The Iliad,* with his principal female protagonist, Helen of Troy, the legendary cause for the tragic Trojan War. Homer does not seek to define her ineffable beauty, and at once we know why. If he were to describe her as a svelte, blue-eyed blonde, that would immediately alienate all the readers who opt for plump, doe-eyed brunettes as the very aesthetic definition of feminine beauty.

Our modern novelists could do learn much from Homer in this regard. He describes the *effect* and *presence* of Helen's ineffable beauty but never her *appearance.* In this respect, the Trojan elders are out by the gates just one day after the Greeks have inflicted heavy losses on their beloved sons. They rue the war; they even suggest giving Helen back to the Greeks in order to terminate the tragic war. They suck in their breaths in their obvious erotic appreciation. They are so stunned by her beauty that they are willing to fight for her to the bitter and embittered end, even if it means the very fall of Troy.

Now the all-important point is that, wisely enough from the poetic view-point, we never define the *appearance* but, rather, only the *essence* of Helen's truly classical beauty. Likewise, in *La Chanson de Roland,* we courteously submit that the real hero of the first magnitude is not Roland but Charlemagne himself, just as Helen of Troy, whom we rarely see in *The Iliad,* was essentially a more powerful protagonist than Andromache, wife of Hector, whom we see far more often. Hence, by analogy, we are concerned in *La Chanson* with Roland in the sense that the action of the drama

1

turns around him and his noble exploits during the French withdrawal from the Saracens through the High Pyrenees. It even assumes an amusing dimension with the *hamartia,* or tragic flaw, of Roland's *hubris,* or pride, or stubbornness. In the end, will Roland, having slain so many countless thousands of Saracens, blow his horn, *sonner son cor,* in an effort to call back Charlemagne's French army in a classic counterattack in which the Christians will surely rout the Saracen infidels? He does. He isn't that vain. But our point is that Charlemagne closes the action, reappears, assumes our poetic attention in a kind of metaphysical dimension: with Roland's death: and thus with the Christian's eternal rebirth for Christ Crucified.

What sort of man is Charlemange? Historically, he was a giant, even a physical giant from a literal six feet to a poeticized seven feet, certainly a legend in his own time. He was the great King of the Franks, both East Franks (French) and West Franks (Germans); the latter called him Karl der Grosse. His presence filled an epoch, and he was one of the few men called *magne* (great) in his own lifetime. Curiously enough, by repute, he could scarcely read or write, but he was emphatically a genius of the first magnitude: a genius, yes, and, above all, a great warrior in the mighty lineage of Alexander, whom the Christians called "great" but whom his own Hellenists called "God." This, then, in essence, is the man we shall be dealing with in our effort to intuit what he was truly like and why his august presence was always behind the French *chansons de geste,* no less than King Arthur was behind the Camelot saga all the way to Lord Tennyson and Edwin Arlington Robinson.

History actually records that at the cataclysmic Battle of Hastings, Taillefer the Jongleur strode out in front of the Norman army, throwing his mighty sword in the air and chanting the entire *Chanson de Roland.* We do not really believe that this anecdote, thoroughly a part of British history, not to say Anglo-Saxon oral tradition, could possibly be apocryphal. It admirably depicts the Norman character, which was to become such an integral part of the British national character when it triumphantly merged in at first a master-slave relationship with that of the Anglo-Saxon after the Battle of Hastings in 1066. Hence, even the jonglery, so to speak, assumes a religious dimension in what was truly a spiritual crusade as much as a political campaign. In a spiritual sense, therefore, this is a profoundly moral tale, organized around the immortal King Charlemagne as our Christian tragic hero.

La Chanson de Roland, in a Christian sense, is a feudalistic story, thus also a Christian story, since feudalism was a profoundly Christian social system, in which the coronation of the king was almost the eighth sacrament.

In legal form and custom, at that time, subordinates were called vassals, and they did homage to their lords, who, in turn, revered the king as head of the temporal state (in theory, though not in actuality for many centuries), just as the pope was then supreme in the spiritual domain as the vicar of Christ on earth. Yet a vassal is more than a mere serf, and the homage is really an etherealized homage, an attitude and posture worthy of a man to his fellow man in Catholic *caritas* (love) and *koinonia* (community).

Thus the first feudal feeling of vassal for lord was intensely patriotic, though rather international (like the Catholic Church) and not at all nationalistic, since nationalism and Protestantism (as George Bernard Shaw argues so well in *Saint Joan*) were the "twin heresy" of Saint Joan of Arc, the reason why she was burned at the stake. Moreover, vassalage is complacent, even proud, but never haughty, and thus something of a Christian virtue: submission to the state: submission to God revealed through the state. The vassal, as throughout *La Chanson de Roland,* is encouraged to be as proud of his vassalage as the lord of his lordship. Consequently, Charlemagne's lowest squire is, in the Christian sense, equal to the great king himself. Indeed, even in *La Chanson de Roland,* perhaps we can best substitute the word "chivalry" for "vassalage."

La Chanson de Roland protrays its Christian heroes as existentialist men of action. For his faith, Archbishop Turpin takes a Christian delight in hacking the Muslim chief from rib to rib. In response, the Christian army of Charlemagne, beholding the deed, truly a spiritual *auto-da-fé,* ever against the infidel, cries aloud with pride that he has executed his existential option as a man of the cloth for the temporal glory of God. They want their Cross to be safe with the archbishop, himself also a mighty warrior, as in Catholic tradition warriors can and should be men of God even when they maim and mutilate and rape and slaughter. There are no conscientious objectors in the heady *Chanson de Roland.* All are existential heroes, making their options for Catholic Christianity against "perfidious Islam."

To return to our story of Taillefer the Jongleur—what, etymologically, is a jongleur anyway but a juggler? No less a man than Saint Francis of Asisi called his monks the jugglers of God. Within the armor of *La Chanson de Roland* there is ever a Christian heart rushing as wildly as within the monastic gown. Moreover, this jongleur in front of William the Conqueror's Norman army, while desiring and even lusting for victory, was screaming out the greatest glorification of failure (Roland's, through his *hubris* and in his stubbornness) ever known in Occidental literature, not excluding the *Götterdämmerung* of the *Nibelungenlied.* What greater truth could they know as the Christians of William the Conqueror than that the court poet was celebrating Roland the Conquered in the greatest epic of all about Charlemagne?

From the standpoint of poetic craftsmanship there is a high note of forlorn hope (existential despair with the *engagement*) in a desperate battle between desperate men in high stakes for the religious future, viz., a Christian kingdom ultimately south of the Pyrenees. The *dénouement,* then, is gloriously inconclusive: tragic: depicting Roland as a Christian tragic hero: tragic, yes, because stubbornly he resisted the call to camaraderie (*caritas* in *koinonia*) that alone would have saved his valiant soldiers: tragic, too, yes, for Charlemagne, and especially for Charlemagne, as the archetypal Christian tragic hero of this singular poem, because he arrives, symbolically, too late: surely indicating that the social system at best only imperfectly serves the spiritual realm of God's Kingdom, the Power, and the Glory.

What does the *dénouement* to *La Chanson de Roland* signify? First, it portrays Charlemagne as tragic Christian emperor establishing his empire in the specious tranquility of total social turmoil, viscosity, existential "thinginess," in which Christian men and women are tragic because they cannot extricate themselves from it: life: hell. Yet, truly, Charlemagne has also executed temporal justice in a temporal way. Thus, truly, he can sleep upon his throne at Aix-la-Chapelle with the beatific peace of a Christian's Paradise on a sober and stark earth. In that day, the Angel of God comes to him to tell him, as if in a trance, that his arms are needed anew in a distant land. Hence, he must opt for Christianity and fight to the end of his days, though his heart is really with Frankish culture and Alcuin's schools. So what happens in one of the greatest dream scenes and political stanzas of all time of a Christian tragic hero in his existential despair and with his existential nausea?

Charlemagne tears his long white beard. He bemoans his restless life as an emperor, totally devoid of the Christianity he craves as a monk in a cell or as a scribe at his bench laboriously copying lost tomes. How could the poem more effectively be Christian than as with Charlemagne the Christian tragic hero's vision of ceaseless campaigns against the infidels, especially since that vision is lamentably true? That war, as the great Catholic critic G.K. Chesterton noted in his introduction to C.K. Scott Moncrieff's admirable translation of *The Song of Roland*, has never ended, will not end in our time, cannot end till under the Great White Throne of God's judgment (in the infinite mercy, compassion, love, *caritas* in the *koinonia* of the New Jerusalem) the Kingdom, the Power, and the Glory at last subdue Satan's "present evil aeon" (as the Church Fathers originally and cogently called it) of the World, the Flesh, and the Devil. For what is Christianity but sanity, and what is evil but discord, as in Milton's Pandemonium as the very citadel of Hell?

Since the discovery of the Oxford manuscript of *La Chanson de Roland,* the academic world has been inundated with material about this epic poem. There is no need for us to attempt an annotated bibliography, since ours is an interpretative, highly impressionistic, and probably quite heretical essay. Yet we must signal Professor Joseph J. Duggan's *The Song of Roland: Formulaic Style and Poetic Craft* as being especially praiseworthy and valuable, indeed, even indispensable, not only for its many abstruse textual emendations, but also (and, to our mind, more importantly) for its many novel aesthetic observations. Of course, we ever need to understand a literary document in the context of its times and culture. In this sense, French literature has been blessed with more admirable and even exquisite and sometimes gamey histories than any other literature, not excluding the classical Greek and Roman. Still, we would like to signal a recent monograph of pertinent value, *A Literary History of France: The Middle Ages,* by Professor John Fox of the University of Exeter, England. Almost as an afterthought, we would like to add that we find the British studies of *La Chanson de Roland* more satisfactory than the American, since under the influence of the novelist Ernest Hemingway and the rather misguided *MLA Style Sheet,* American academia has plunged feet first into the Miltonic pandemonium of pure journalism and, at its worst, journalese—and without the panegyrics, too. For a traditional view of *La Chanson de Roland,* we refer the reader to L. Cazamian's *A History of French Literature,* which may be dated but which is analytically if not synthetically cogent.

In our opinion, every aspect of *La Chanson de Roland* has been admirably or execrably studied and even overstudied, including "la belle Aude," whose love for Roland gets all of four lines in the epic—every aspect, that is to say, except Charlemagne, since he appears only obliquely and almost anticlimactically in the *dénouement.* He deserves our interpretation, and we return to him in summary of his appearance as a Christian tragic hero in his own right. Let him speak for himself through Captain Moncrieff's worthy translation, *The Song of Roland:*

Here is the cosmic plan in which Charlemagne is the hub of the wheel:

> *For Charlemagne a great marvel God planned:*
> *Making the sun still in his course to stand.*
> *So pagans fled, and chased them well the Franks*
> *Through the Valley of Shadows, close in hand;*
> *Towards Sarraguce by force they chased them back,*

And as they went with killing blows attacked:
Barred their highways and every path they had.
The River Sebre before them reared its bank,
'Twas very deep, marvellous current ran;
No barge thereon nor dromond nor caland.
A god of theirs invoked they, Tervagant.
And then leaped in, but there no warrant had.
The armèd men more weighty were for that,
Many of them down to the bottom sank,
Downstream the rest floated as they might hap;
So much water the luckiest of them drank,
That all were drowned, with marvellous keen pangs.
"An evil day," cry Franks,
"ye saw Rollant!"

(CLXXX)

Here is the weakness and strength of Charlemagne, the physical weakness after a great battle, buttressed by his great Christian strength through his existential will to believe.

That Emperour is lying in a mead;
By 's head, so brave, he's placed his mighty spear;
On such a night unarmed he will not be.
He's donned his white hauberk, with broidery,
Has laced his helm, jewelled with golden beads,
Girt on Joiuse, there never was its peer,
Whereon each day thirty fresh hues appear.
All of us know that lance, and well may speak
Whereby Our Lord was wounded on the Tre:
Charles, by God's grace, possessed its point of steel!
His golden hilt he enshrined it underneath.
By that honour and by that sanctity
The name Joiuse was for that sword decreed.
Barons of France may not forgetful be
Whence comes the ensign "Monjoie," they cry at need;
Wherefore no race against them can succeed.

(CLXXXIII)

Here is the first vision:

Charles, like a man worn out with labour, slept.

Saint Gabriel the Lord to him hath sent,
Whom as a guard o'er the Emperour He set;
Stood all night long that angel by his head.
In a vision announced he to him then
A Battle, should be fought against him yet,
Significance of griefs demonstrated.
Charlès looked up towards the sky, and there
Thunders and winds and blowing gales beheld,
And hurricanes and marvellous tempests;
Lightnings and flames he saw in readiness,
That speedily on all his people fell;
Apple and ash, their spear-shafts all burnèd,
Also their shields, e'en the golden bosses,
Crumbled the shafts of their trenchant lances,
Crushed their hauberks and all their steel helmets.
His chevaliers he saw in great distress.
Bears and leopards would feed upon them next;
Adversaries, dragons, wyverns, serpents,
Griffins were there, thirty thousand, no less,
Nor was there one but on some Frank it set.
And the Franks cried: "Ah! Charlemagne, give help!"
(CLXXXV)

Here, in the second vision, is Meaning for the Cosmos, in which Charlemagne is to continue to opt existentially for the Power, the Kingdom, and the Glory against the World, the Flesh, and the Devil of the Infidels:

And, after that, another vision came:
Him seemed in France, at Aix, on a terrace,
And that he held a bruin by two chains;
Out of Ardenne saw thirty bears that came,
And each of them words, as a man might, spake:
Said to him: "Sire, give him to us again!
It is not right that he with you remain,
He's of our kin, and we must lend him aid."
A harrier fair ran out of his palace,
Among them all the greatest bear assailed
On the green grass, beyond his friends some way.
There saw the King marvellous give and take;
But he knew not which fell, nor which o'ercame.
The angel of God so much to him made plain.

> *Charlès slept on till the clear dawn of day.*
>
> *(CLXXXVI)*

Christian concern is emphatically explicit, is it not? In a word, we should not be surprised. For a generation *Beowulf* was analyzed only as a Germanic and pagan document, according to Professor Kemp Malone and his powerful (if not omnipotent) school of thought at Johns Hopkins University. But Professor Raymond Carter Sutherland has added, rightly too, that *Beowulf* not only has Christian elements but is also something of a Christian document, in which the Norse gods were certainly Christianized by Christian storytellers of a later date and in another place. Likewise, *La Chanson de Roland,* we submit, is a profoundly Christian document; and we must never overlook its *caritas* and *koinonia* and humility in the *gesta* of its *beau geste* ideology of existential action.

Too, the oblique appearance of the incomparable Charlemagne is ever near the center of our attention, especially in the beginning and at the *dénouement.* He is the most Christian protagonist of the poem, and regrettably the epic's Christian dimensions are all too often forgotten, overlooked, almost deliberately ignored for pagan concerns. But if we miss the salient fact of *La Chanson de Roland* as a spiritual poem, we miss the ultimate meaning of the epic itself. Surely, the theme is that one never acts alone in *koinonia,* as Roland did, but rather must meaningfully opt for *caritas* in camaraderie: for salvation. And whatever else our little essay may or may not have done, the epic turns upon Charlemagne as the Christian tragic hero (who opts for Spirit but must act in Flesh) as surely as God's earth revolves around God's sun in an ordered Cosmos, where angels and men and demons all have their properly assigned hierarchical places in God's great Chain of Being.

Montaigne as Christian Tragic Hero

Is Montaigne truly the skeptic of all skeptics, as the critical world claims, or is he rather a deeply committed Christian, committed to Catholicism at that, as we maintain? This is, indeed, the knotty problem we shall attempt to resolve. Moreover, we shall attempt to resolve it, in our existential moment of eternal time, by analyzing and synthesizing Montaigne as the Christian tragic hero that so clearly emerges from our consideration of his unique *Essais*.

There is a wealth of material on Montaigne, much and indeed most of it worthwhile, though some of it is platitudinous drivel like Marcel Tétel's *Montaigne,* a regrettable popularization of a complex man. In French criticism, we particularly want to signal out Alexandre Micha's *Le Singulier Montaigne* and Jean Plattard's *Montaigne et son temps,* truly an admirable study. At the same time, we do not wish to forget Pierre Moreau's *Montaigne: L'Homme et l'Oeuvre,* one study in the remarkable series, "Connaissance des Lettres," surely an informative series for French literature. In American criticism, Ralph Waldo Emerson's essay "Montaigne; or, the Skeptic," from his *Representative Men: Seven Lectures,* is much cited, though we wonder why. With its aphoristic sentences, totally devoid of form and quite divorced from contiguous style, it is a masterful revelation of Ralph Waldo Emerson, almost without reference to its singular subject, the enigmatic yet simplistic Michel de Montaigne.

In contemporary America, however, we do have a distinguished professor who admirably intuits and apprehends his subject. Professor Donald M. Frame's *Montaigne's Discovery of Man: The Humanization of a Humanist* is the finest analysis we have ever read of our subject, whether in English, French, or any other language. His *Montaigne: A Biography* is truly a remarkable re-creation (with its radical reorientation) of a most remarkable

Renaissance man. In deference to Professor Frame, we have used his English translation, *The Complete Essays of Montaigne,* since Montaigne's French is so baroque and involuted that it proves difficult for modern readers, even (for that matter) to well-educated and sophisticated Frenchmen. For those who do not like their cordials diluted, we refer them to the headier original liqueur of the *Essais* of the universal and immortal Montaigne, who (as we maintain) will live through his essential Catholicism and not at all through the scepticism which certain superficial critics have rather wrongly ascribed to him.

Skepticism, as we know, at least in a sense, is the leit-motif in our understanding of Montaigne. "Que sçais-je?" is the *devise* to our apprehension of Montaigne: or, solipsistically, what do I know, what can I ever know, except my own sense impressions of my own ego through my own ego? Indeed, it is tragic that this motto, extracted from the "Apology for Raymond Sebond," has been understood as the basis for a "skeptical attack upon religion," whereas in *reality* Montaigne uses his solipsism—truly, his Christian existentialism—in defense of the historic Catholic faith. In actuality, Montaigne posits his Christian system on doubt, rooted in existential despair, while Pascal posits his system on the "pari," or wager, or *engagement,* or self-conscious commitment to Catholic Christianity to believe in his initial existential option.

In a very real sense, Montaigne's intellectual life (and that is what properly interests us) begins only with his retirement to his family château in Bordeaux on his thirty-eighth birthday. His Epicurean period has ended. That is not to say that Montaigne was ever a hedonist *farouche,* a determined and self-determined pleasure-seeker and *débauché.* Instead, he was a sensualist in the grand manner of Epicurus himself, for whom are important the attenuated pleasures of wine, a woman, a good book, excellent conversation, a pleasant interlude with carnal love, and then, most of all, high philosophy (or solace in the *post coitum triste*) to make life meaningful. After all, Montaigne was enigmatically, also problematically, pagan and even Stoic, and so he subscribed to Aristotle's "golden mean" of moderation in all things, even and especially in the metaphysical dimensions of historic Epicureanism.

Here, in his home, beginning his immortal and sometimes interminable essays, he makes his first existential option, toward the Catholic faith, through Christian doubt (or, as we should say, intellectual reservation), in the thinginess of the World, the Flesh, and the Devil. He defines his goal. Clearly, emphatically, he states that goal for himself, to himself, since the *Essais* are primarily a document in self-communication and only secondarily imply communication with interested readers:

> There is nothing with which I have at all ages more occupied my
> mind than with images of death. Even in the most licentious
> season of my age . . . amid ladies and games, someone would
> think me involved in digesting some jealousy by myself, or the
> uncertainty of some hope, while I was thinking about I don't
> remember whom, who had been overtaken a few days before by a
> hot fever and by death, on leaving a similar feast, his head full of
> idleness, love, and a happy time, like myself; and that the same
> chance was hanging from my ear. . . . I did not wrinkle my
> forehead any more over that thought than any other . . . . Other-
> wise for my part I would have been in continual fear and frenzy;
> for never did a man so distrust his life, never did a man set less
> faith in his duration.

In itself, this is an excellent definition of Renaissance humanism, in which
Montaigne so amply participated. As he says later (and Stoically) in his
admirable essay "To Philosophize Is to Learn to Die," life is really a preparation for the ultimate reality of death; and the wise man will seek only to
die swiftly without pain.

Professor Frame points out, significantly enough, that it is only after the
Saint Bartholomew's Day Massacre that Montaigne assumes his skeptical
pose, which, in reality may be only that—a philosophical pose, also a risible
posture, since we see him as a profoundly committed Catholic. The Stoics
are concerned about doing well (making the right existential options) in this
life. Yet, since Stoical humanism ignores or suppresses the fundamental
contrary nature of man (original sin), Montaigne devoutly and somewhat
dumbly feels the pressing need for an indefinable more. He situates this, too,
in Catholicism, where the Christian makes existential options not for his
body in a social context, as the Stoic does, but rather, more meaningfully, for
his immortal soul in a spiritual cosmos. Significantly, in this regard, Montaigne writes:

> Out of a thousand, there is not one [soul] that is straight and com-
> posed at any moment of its life; and it might be doubted whether
> according to its natural condition it can ever be so. But as for
> combining this with constancy, that is the soul's ultimate perfec-
> tion; I mean even if nothing should jar it. . . . Let him be as wise
> as he please, after all he is a man: what is there more vulnerable,

more wretched and more null? Wisdom does not overcome our natural conditions. He must blink his eyes at the blow that threatens him; he must shudder if you plant him on the edge of a precipice. He pales with fear, he reddens with shame; he moans at the colic. . . . Enough for him to curb and moderate his inclinations; for to do away with them is not in him.

("Drunkenness," II: 2)

Here, certainly, skepticism is in full flower. At the same time, we do not interpret Montaigne's skepticism in a negative sense. It is not at all, as certain naïve critics have vainly presumed, a question that precludes a positive answer. Instead, as an existentialist option, as a Catholic *engagement* itself, it is a question that hopes for, and even suggests within its proper limits, a meaningful answer in the measured history of Catholic Christianity.

"The Apology for Raymond Sebond" is that part of the *Essais* upon which the other smaller parts hang and from which they can never be properly dissociated. What, in a word, is the subject of the essay? It is not really about the critics of Sebond, as it purports to be, since they are mentioned only occasionally and vaguely. Rather, this most significant essay is about the follies of the ancient dogmatic philosophers. In it, Montaigne savagely counterattacks: If man would only accept the Christian truth that all human wisdom is mere folly in the eyes of God, then this argument, surely an act of philosophical supererogation, would be quite unnecessary. But, hélas, man is far too vain in his unweening spiritual pride, itself the *hamartia* of original sin, to entertain this essentially Christian position:

> Presumption is our natural and original malady. The most vulnerable and frail of all creatures is man, and at the same time, says Pliny, the most arrogant. He feels and sees himself lodged here, amid the mire and dung of the world . . . and in his imagination he goes planting himself above the circle of the moon and bringing the sky down beneath his feet. It is by the vanity of this same imagination that he equals himself to God, that he attributes to himself divine characteristics, that he picks himself out and separates himself from the horde of other creatures.

In a word, what is life to the Christian–hope or fear? Perhaps even the Christian hero has more to fear, particularly in terms of eternal damnation. Yet, at the same time, apprehension, which Montaigne sees at first "historically and spiritually necessary," in reality does far more harm than good, as the following lines clearly indicate:

When real evils fail us, knowledge lends us hers. . . . Compare the life of a man enslaved to such imaginings with that of a plowman letting himself follow his natural appetites, measuring things only by the present taste of them, without knowledge and without prognostication, and who has pain only when he has it, whereas the other often has the stone in his soul before he has it in his loins. As if he were not in time to suffer the pain when he is in it, he anticipates it in imagination and runs to meet it.

Moreover, is knowledge always good? Should man not recognize the spiritual danger of the *libido sciendi?* Wasn't this the original sin of Adam and Eve in the Garden of Eden? Indeed, this was the beginning of the end in the decline and fall of the human race. As the Bible reiterates, pride is our *hamartia,* our fatal flaw, our "mole of nature," in the Greek sense. It is even out of pride that we try to limit and otherwise circumscribe God, though our concepts do not even apply to him:

It is for God alone to interpret his works and to know himself. . . . Our faith is not of our own acquiring, it is a pure present of another's liberality. It is not by reasoning or by our understanding that we have received our religion; it is by external authority and command. The weakness of our judgment helps us more in this than its strength, and our blindness more than our clearsightedness. It is the mediation of our ignorance more than of the knowledge that we are learned with that divine learning. . . . Let us bring to it nothing of our own but obedience and submission.

Throughout the essay, Montaigne seems to waver, emphatically tempted by the Stoicism that he officially denounces. In the end, however, he says that an aspiration for Stoical humanism is quite pointless:

There is not truer saying in all his stoical school than that one. But to make the handful bigger than the hand, the armful bigger than the arm, and to hope to straddle more than the reach of our legs, is impossible and unnatural. Nor can man raise himself above himself and humanity; for he can see only with his own eyes, and seize only with his own grasp. He will rise, if God lends him his hand; he will rise by abandoning and renouncing his own means, and letting himself be raised and uplifted by divine grace; but not otherwise.

At last, Montaigne has taken his firm stand for Catholicism, though his existential option was always implicit in his original posture of a truly Christ-oriented and Christ-centered skepticism. For Montaigne was never a sophist in the Greek etymological sense. Rather, in the Catholic sense, he was merely a "Doubting Thomas" with his loaded questions in solipsistic skepticism. And we remember glady that Thomas, too, for all his doubts, also found Christ: and, through Christ and in Christ, salvation.

The *Essais* are a long philosophical and headily spiritual descent, *de profundis,* into self-discovery for the express purpose of liberation of self, psyche, and soul: Christian ego, without the pejorative connotations. Within this remarkable cerebral "voyage into the mind and the Christian intellect," there is a certain "Happy Paradox," as Professor Frame aptly calls it. In other words, it is the alliance between ignorance and happiness, surely a Christian doctrine but hardly a classically pagan concept. In fact, is the mechanism of our knowledge a guarantee of happiness as well as of ignorance?

The resolution to this pregnant question can best be understood in terms of "ordeal and triumph." The ordeal had its physical dimensions for Montaigne, for while he had been admirably healthy till he was forty, he never knew a moment's well-being afterward. At the same time, as the Greeks well knew, "pain is gain," and it metamorphoses man, or, rather, cannot metamorphose him, through the spiritual dimensions of physical suffering. Hence, suddenly almost inexplicably, Montaigne actually becomes an *optimist.* In "The Education of Children," he finds the ineffable beauty of the consolation of philosophy, which as a humanist he interprets as Stoicism, but which as a Catholic he ever interprets (rightly, in our opinion as Catholic critics) as Christianity:

> The soul in which Philosophy dwells should by its health make even the body healthy. It should make its contentment, tranquillity, and gladness shine out from within; should form in its own mold the outward demeanor, and consequently furnish it with graceful pride, an active and joyous bearing, and equable and good-natured countenance. It is *Baroco* and *Baralipton* that make their disciples wretched and grimy, and not Philosophy: they know her only by hearsay. Why, her business is to calm the tempests of the soul and to teach hunger and fevers to laugh—not by some imaginary epicycles but by crude, workable, and palpable reasons. . . . It is Philosophy that teaches us to live.

What is the fundamental nature of free men? In religious terms, man, or the Christian hero, by definition a Christian hero in terms of the World, the Flesh, and the Devil, defines himself in a cosmic context of good and evil. In this sense, indeed, Montaigne is an avowed Christian. But Montaigne is an artist as well as a man. In this sense, therefore, as a writer, he defines himself in terms of the dynamic tension of nature versus art.

Still, what, is nature? As he always maintains, there are only two main tenets. First, whatever is found in other living creatures is natural. Second, whatever makes for our happiness is natural. Moreover, the two criteria find a certain almost surrealist unity in the obvious fact that all creatures seek happiness—at least, in terms of sense gratification. Wisely perhaps, but only perhaps, at least for the artist or the jaded decadent of the eternal Byzantium, nature recognizes and accepts us for what we truly are in the bones, blood, sinews, fibers, and visceral organs.

Yet, enigmatically, perhaps more problematically, art refuses to accept us (at least as creatures of circumstance) in our human condition. In this context, how does Montaigne, as his own Christian tragic hero, reject Stoicism? It is because Stoicism is profoundly antinatural. As a philosophy, it orders us to conquer instincts with which nature has endowed us. Can man change his own essential being? Can even the existentialist (perhaps a Catholic existentialist like Montaigne) hope to change his essential being—or, rather, as we are inclined to think, only reorient it?

Analogously, has art led us astray from nature? And if so, is art to that extent anti-Christian? No less a philosopher than Plato thought that, indeed, it was immoral. Most of the time, Montaigne, in the lineage of Plato, tends to deprecate art—at least, in dimensions of Théophile Gautier and Oscar Wilde's "art for art's sake." The praise of nature increases, and in time it becomes a rather monotonous leitmotif of Montaigne's skeptical philosophy, which, enigmatically, has profound Christian and also Catholic dimensions.

In "Of Cannibals," Montaigne tells about a tribe of Brazilian Indians in terms that foreshadow nineteenth-century Romanticism in their appreciation of the Noble Savage:

> They are wild, just as we call wild the fruits that nature has produced by herself and in her natural course; whereas really it is those that we have changed artificially and led astray from the common order that we should rather call wild. In the former the genuine, most useful, and natural virtues and properties are alive and vigorous, which we have debased in the latter, and have only adapted them to the pleasure of our corrupted taste. . . . It is not reasonable that art should win the place of honor over our great

and powerful mother nature. We have so overloaded the beauty
and richness of her works by our inventions that we have quite
smothered her. Yet wherever she shines forth in her purity, she
wonderfully puts to shame our vain and frivolous attempts . . . . All
our efforts cannot even succeed in reproducing the nest of the tiniest
little bird, its contexture, its beauty and convenience; nor even
the web of the puny and vile spider.

These nations, then, seem to be barbarous in this sense, that
they have been fashioned very little by the human mind, and are
still very close to their original naturalness. The laws of nature
still rule them, very little corrupted by ours.

Montaigne makes his existential option for nature, not for art. Moreover,
as he cogently argues, do we not surpass the savages in the very degree of our
"civilized barbarities"? Still, it is not only instinct or custom that gives them
these qualities; it is also, and even more importantly, reasoning and judgment.

Nature, however, must not be a tyrant. As a Catholic, Montaigne could
never agree with Alexander Pope, a deist, who wrote, rather cruelly: "Whatever is, is right." For art, like philosophy (and art is, in a sense, philosophy),
consoles man in the existential despair he feels when entrapped in the
"thinginess' of the human condition. He seems to imply that art, while
secondary, can yet be healthful, salubrious, and not degenerate into the
baroque decadence of the goldsmiths of Byzantium. But what he is clearly
leading into is a higher human naturalness that is beyond art in and of itself.
After all, as a diversion, art is, for the most part, merely the benefit of
our inconstancy.

What, then, can we conclude about Montaigne's perceptions of human
nature? First, as a child of nature, man is a prodigal son who belongs at
home, though he has strayed in the domains of art and abstract intellect. He
is made of soul, though the body lamentably tends to forget it. He is kinetic,
constantly developing, changing, metamorphosing. Man, in the end, becomes great only when he recognizes and accepts his limitations. Hence, the
Christian tragic hero is transfigured into a saint when he accepts and deals
with his body and accommodates it to his self, psyche, soul, incorporating
the World, the Flesh, and the Devil into the Kingdom, the Power, and the
Glory, just as the mystic always incorporates himself into the cosmos (and
the Christian mystic into the Christian cosmos), while the "merely mysterious" somewhat osmotically absorbs the whole cosmos into his puny self,
psyche, soul.

The soul of the Christian tragic hero can and must rule the Dionysian passions of the body, as man's baser self, as nature that is lower than nature. He can even accept the pair of body and being now, as he once welcomed his attenuated Epicurean pleasures. It is his Christian awareness of the strict limits, and limitations, of the Flesh, and thus the World and the Devil, that gives him a surrealist sense of salvation. He now has the saint's power of control over sense impressions. It is precisely this freedom from apprehension that gives him the fullest measure of joy even in the last days of his waning health. In a sense, he takes an almost sadomasochistic delight in the intervals of his waxing and waning health and disease.

Only one key idea remains to be voiced in Montaigne: that of human solidarity and unity, which in the twentieth century Jules Romains cogently codified in his "unanisme," as life in a kind of communistic group-soul. Yet, enigmatically, though not problematically for the Christian, it is his soul, his atomistic soul, that interests him, absorbs him, and even defines him: the atomic particle shot from the atomic gun of all mankind and the cosmos, veering unpredictably to the left or the right according to the theories of quantum mechanics in an uncertainty principle, which, as the Christian knows,—at least the devout Catholic, like Montaigne-is free will and interprets in terms of free will, as we make our existential options for God and the Power and the Glory and the Kingdom, or for Satan and the World, the Flesh, and the Devil.

Montaigne, as a Christian tragic hero, is ever tolerant, never dogmatic. As a matter of fact, he starkly terminated the first edition of the *Essais* with the following lines:

> I do not at all hate opinions contrary to mine. I am so far from
> being vexed to see the discord between my judgments and others',
> and from making myself incompatible with the society of men
> because they are of a different opinion than mine, that on the con-
> trary, since variety is the most general form that nature has
> followed, I find it much more novel and rare to see our humors
> and opinions agree. And perhaps there were never in the world
> two opinions entirely and exactly alike, any more than two faces.
> Their most intrinsic quality is diversity and discord.

His attitude is so compelling that we wish he had kept the passage as the very proper and fitting conclusion of the final edition of the *Essais*. For the words epitomize a Noble Man who, indeed, has been transfigured, metamorphosed, and ennobled by the very texture of his physical, psychological, and spiritual suffering in his metaphysical dimensions as a Christian tragic hero.

Certainly, in his solipsism, later to become literary and artistic impressionism, nobody, starting from "Que sçais-je?", ever discovered himself as fully
and completely as Montaigne. His essays are really a protracted auto-
biography. Indeed, they are even more than that; they are the most intimate
of all diaries, in which a man plumbs the depths of his own mind: and his own
soul. But solipsism, at best, is only an imperfect way to understand the
world, for it never really apprehends it and perhaps only intuits it inchoately.
It remains for man to relate himself to society, to the world, to the cosmos—
in a word, to God—and, as a Christian, therefore a tragic hero, to Christ, as
the Messiah.

Ultimately, Montaigne does relate himself to others (in his exploration of
self and selves) in the travels of his last days, as related in the *Journal*, which
he originally wrote in Italian, though he dropped it for the obvious reason
that he could explain himself incomparably better in his native French. The
Journal is an interesting, even absorbing appendage to the thought of Montaigne. But it is precisely that—only an appendange, nothing more. Montaigne is good in his *Journal,* but as a sedentary man from Bordeaux, he
waxes rhapsodic over the exterior nature of man as he travels. Thus, sadly,
too, it is not the impassioned cry of a creature of circumstance, a Christian
soul on fire, a tragic hero, as he always is in his *Essais*, the most introspective
search for a Stoics's truth laid bare and also a Christian's Truth laid bare
ever made by man.

That, in a word, is why he appeals so irresistibly to us atomized modern
men in our increasingly socialist and group-centered societies. That, too, is
why he appeals in such a spirit of desperate Dionysian desire to the most
introspective of modern continental writers, André Gide, who himself wrote
emphatically though not always well about his chosen hero in introspection,
Michel de Montaigne, a Renaissance man of affairs of Bordeaux as much as
Gide is the son of the Paris, which Montaigne truly preferred.

As his own *honnête homme* in Renaissance formulation of "decorum,"
Montaigne lives for us today, and will continue to live unless he is totally
robotized in a Marxist beehive society, as an expression of Christian wholeness: yes, "totality," since that is the word that best describes him, as like a
Christian mystic he tries to reconcile opposites and harmonize them into a
whole: a totality. It is a mistake to think, as certain naïve critics do, that Montaigne is inconsistent, inconstant, ambivalent, or even ambiguous.

He is none of these. He is always the total man, and is that not the proper
definition of a Christian, for does the Christian not ever aim to embrace (and
also mystically incorporate into himself and incorporate himself in) the

totality of life? Opposites are not truly truly opposites but are, rather, always inextricably interrelated as complementary and not mutually exclusive models of perception. To be sure, the surest way to find goodness and happiness is through wisdom, and Montaigne is nothing if not wise, almost insufferably wise.

But what is wisdom? For Montaigne, it consists entirely in knowing how to live graciously as un *honnête homme* with the exemplary decorum of the golden mean, moderation, surely a Catholic as well as an Aristotelian ideal. It depends on self-knowledge. Both Socrates and Christ, both pagan and Christian, said, "Know thyself," did they not? Montaigne accepts this injunction as law. He obeys it. More importantly, he lives it. Still, one must attempt to know others, too, his Christian brothers, though it is exceedingly difficult. In the end, then, as a climax to his extraordinary life, Montaigne becomes mayor of Bordeaux. He serves his fellow Christians in a Christian society and thus participates in *caritas* in the *koinonia* of his Christian community of a Catholic Bordeaux.

In the end, what remains for us in Montaigne's incomparable message in his sacred quest for self-knowledge, which he equates with salvation? It is joy: yes, joy. Now, certain Christians, most notably the Puritans, feel a *douceur,* a sadness, in this existential confrontation with life. But even Jansenists feel attenuated pleasure, and most Catholics feel a consuming joy, a veritable *joie de vivre,* sometimes incarnate in the carnival season. This is what Montaigne felt in a sensual way as a *libertin* (though not truly libertine or *débauché*) in his early life as a hedonist. Then he knows the joy of his pleasures in a cerebral Epicureanism. Finally, he is drawn to Stoicism, perhaps the ultimate temptation for the noble man in our Christian Era in the Occident.

Joy, yes, joy: This is the essential nature of the Christian. When he knows it, he then ceases to be a tragic hero in the metaphysical dimension, though the World, the Flesh, and the Devil may crush him. Did some of the saints not die with beatific smiles of Christian joy upon their curling lips as the cruel rocks of their tormentors beat out their brains and as the flames of the anti-Christian pyres licked their feet, their hands, their lips, their brows, their brains? Does the study of Catholic hagiography not always substantiate this observation?

This is what we claim for Montaigne: that he was not truly a skeptic, once he made his existential option to try to believe to believe (which is all that the Catholic Church has ever demanded), but rather a Christian saint. To the extent that he suffered to gain Christian insight into himself, his soul, his psyche, he was, of course, a Christian tragic hero. In the end, however, this quarter-Jew, rejecting the ethnocentrism of Judaism and Jewry, opts for Christian joy: exuberance.

And he lives! How he lives! This, essentially, is why we will always read Montaigne despite the complexities of his language, as French increasingly becomes the journalese of *Le Figaro.* We will always clasp Montaigne to our bosom as we read him through the passing years, like a trusted old friend whom we see all too infrequently and only on festive occasions. Like Baudelaire to his "lecteur," we exclaim to Montaigne: "mon semblable, mon frère."

But why do we feel this way when, indeed, as bad Christians, we may never approximate his total vision of Christian life or his exuberant joy in expressing the ineffable beauty of that Christian life? Alas, it is the dark side of Montaigne that we prefer, since we are bad Christians with a shadow side to our spiritual life. As with another Catholic writer in our twentieth century, François Mauriac, a most perceptive psychologist as well as a skilled novelist, we glory in the *faisandage* of Montaigne's gamier moments of doubt and hedonistic decadence.

To our own spiritual horror, itself a *nouveau frisson,* as Victor Hugo wrote of Charles Baudelaire's *Les Fleurs du mal,* we prefer and even relish our Montaigne as a Christian tragic hero of social and cosmic suffering, not as a transfigured soul on Mount Purgatory ready to ascend into heaven, because at those moments he most totally resembles us in our existential despair and nausea as we writhe (trying to opt for good and not evil) in the existential "thinginess" from which we try vainly and perhaps vaingloriously to extricate ourselves: for ourselves: most of all, for the God whom we wish not only to worship but also to embrace.

Pascal as Christian Tragic Hero

Let us outrage the very proper canons of literary tradition at the outset by claiming that Blaise Pascal is the most preposterously overrated writer, philosopher, and even scientist in Occidental history. As a writer, he has been called the first modern stylist because he eschews Latin cadences in favor of an assumed simplicity. As for ourselves, we deride this as Rimbaldian descent into journalism and even jounalese; at its best, it represents the end result of *Le Figaro* and *L'Humanité*, and not for political reasons, either. Furthermore, Pascal was never a schematized philosopher in his *Pensées* but rather only a keen aphoristic observer of the human condition, though not nearly so perceptive as Friedrich Nietzsche in his far more profoundly philosophical *Thus Spake Zarathustra* and *Beyond Good and Evil*. Even worse, Pascal, at his best, was far more a technician than a pure scientist; he would never be considered by the impartial observer as a Newton or Leibnitz. So, as we regret to say, for existentially absurb reasons, Blaise Pascal is the most preposterously overrated man of all time in our own Judeo-Christian Occidental tradition.

Lucien Goldmann has made a kind of critical splash on Pascal in his almost totally erroneous *The Hidden God: A Study of Tragic Vision in the "Pensées" of Pascal and the Tragedies of Racine*. It is simply that, being unfamiliar with the niceties of Christian theology, Goldmann apprehends the "Aristotelian tragedy" but never the "Catholic tragedy." Hence his highly schematized tome, venerable by critics in our own time, is almost totally worthless. Fortunat Strowski's *Pensées de Pascal*, however, is far more satisfactory, and it shows a far greater promise of impartial critical longevity. Sister Marie Louise Hubert's *Pascal Unfinished Apology* is rather sympathetic, especially coming from a Catholic nun, for Pascal at his best was a Protestant, and a Jansenist at that, trying rather vainly to pass himself off as a devout practicing Catholic (which he truly never was) within the Roman communion. Emile Cailliet's *Pascal: The Emergence of Genius* shows its genuine moments of real perception. Hence, we recommend it highly, though not quite without reservations. Jan Miel's *Pascal and Theology* is really very close to the center of our spiritual interests, and thus we recommend it highly. But in the American ethos, and as American Catholics, we find Morris Bishop particularly appreciative, first in his *Blaise Pascal* and then in his *Pascal: The Life of Genius.* If we cancel out the ecstatic moments of his rather puritanical enthusiasm, we can come to a real appreciation and apprehension of the true Pascal, who was, we fear, the most limited philosopher, spiritualist, and mystic in Occidental Christian history.

Most tragically, Blaise Pascal tries to pass himself off as an orthodox Catholic despite his close alliance with the Jansenists of Port-Royal, or, as they really were, Protestants (and even Puritans at that) within the Catholic Communion. It was the Abbé de Saint-Cyran who confessed the nuns at Port-Royal. This extraordinary Basque studied at the University of Louvain, the European center of neo-Stoicism, and learned to relate Christianity to the classical Stoicism of Zeno, Epictetus, and the immortal Marcus Aurelius.

While at Louvain, he knotted a close friendship with Cornelius Jansen, a young Fleming, who influenced him profoundly by his interpretation of personal holiness in the long lineage of Saint Augustine. They spent five years in Saint Cyran's home at Bayonee, but ultimately Jansen returned to Louvain and later became Bishop of Ypres. Jansen wrote a three-thousand page book entitled *Augustinius,* the gospel of Jansenism, which tried to systematize the teachings of Saint Augustine as the essential message of Catholic Christianity.

It was Antoine Arnauld, doctor of the Sorbonne, who captained the Jansenist sect in Paris, to which Pascal belonged and to which he gave all the waning energy of his latter years. Ultimately, of course, his position was crushed by the Vatican through the Jesuits, who represented the center of Catholicism. As a scientist—or rather, really a technocrat—Pascal perhaps was drawn to Jansenism through its special appeal to him for its *esprit de géométrie,* which he apprehended as a budding Christian mystic through the *esprit de finesse,* the two categories of understanding that Pascal brilliantly codified. In time, through his alliance with Port-Royal, Pascal came to worship a stern and harsh and even unloving God of granite, very foreign to a tolerant God of Catholic love and Catholic reconciliation.

Indeed, the most important point in Pascal's religious system is profoundly Protestant rather than Catholic. We refer, of course, to his "pari," or wager, which Pascal formulates from his theory of chance and probability. As a Protestant would say, Pascal opted for probability: that probably there was a God, and in that event one should wager on his existence. A Catholic, on the other hand, would initially give intellectual assent to belief, or even simply try to believe, for that is all the Catholic Church has historically ever asked of the sincere Christian: in modern terms, to make a Christian *engagement* in terms of that first existential option, itself very much a Catholic existential option.

We wonder, in sober truth, why so much has been made of the "pari." It is truly unworthy of the Christian, who, as we hope, is not a rash gambler, though we readily admit that spiritual man is quite consumed by existential anguish in his existential despair and with his existential nausea. In short, Pascal's wager is a rather specious rationalization of an assumed rationalism. Besides, Pascal did not invent the sacred quest for the "hidden God," *le dieu caché,* or the *deus absconditus.* The concept is firmly rooted in Stoicism, which has contributed so ineffably much to the richness of Christianity, especially Catholic Christianity. For Catholics have always been embarked on the holy quest, as if for the Holy Grail, of the "Hidden God," or the *deus absconditus.*

Les Lettres provinciales, a much overrated document in the literary sense and an unfair one in the religious sphere, dates from January 1656, when Arnauld called upon the young Pascal to write in the defense of Jansenism. The polemical case of Jesuits versus Jansenists was one of the most important crises in French intellectual history. Though himself a scholar, Pascal rebelled against the idea of scholasticism, which the Jesuits so eagerly and devoutly embraced. With his constitutional distrust and even burning hatred of everything Jesuitical, Pascal particularly fought the order on the doctrine of free will, a cardinal tenet of orthodox Christianity. Pascal found the idea "unscientific," as he argued, though in truth it was essentially a Calvinist doctrine coming out in his Protestant Jansenism. Free will, according to Pascal in his *Lettres provinciales,* means that an action has no cause other than itself, though few Catholics would agree with this novel interpretation. Pascal felt that this traditional emphasis on free will meant that it had actually taken the place of the universal will. What does this mean? In Catholic terms, good works were totally deemphasized, for man could attain salvation only through the grace of God.

Throughout *Les Lettres provinciales,* which had historical impact but little inherent value, Pascal ever begged the question. He ridiculed the doctors of the Sorbonne for being overly subtle on weighty matters, and he implied that the man of good sense could readily resolve the tedious argument of learned fools. With his journalistic style (was journalism ever a good style?), Pascal had a great impact upon the general public of his time, which, indeed, was not overly sophisticated or aesthetic. He accused the Jesuits of forming a cabal. In actuality, it was the Jansenist cabal of Port-Royal that had initiated the suicidal cabal. He accused the Jesuits of attacking, though in actuality (again) it had been the Janenists of Port-Royal who had first attacked. Pascal's delight in the cabal was so great that he actually "hid out" at a Paris inn under the *nom de guerre* of M. de Mons, like a little boy playing at cops and robbers.

Viciously, Pascal then began to attack "Jesuit immorality and double-dealing." In so doing, as with his calculated misinterpretation of the Jesuit position on "reservations," Pascal perverted the very doctrine of the confessional, where "the case," rather than the abstract rule, was always the burning central concern. The Jesuits had invented nothing new with their casuistry, which, in truth, had always been at the very heart of the Catholic confessional. Clearly, we feel that Pascal, as a Protestant, even a Puritan, was trying to get away from the sacrament of confession, except to God alone and without the priest in individual privacy, as the Calvinists and the Lutherans insisted on doing.

Moreover, in perverting the Jesuit points of theology, Pascal misrepresented himself in the "interests of fair play." As a matter of fact, it was he who waxed overly subtle, while the Jesuit pronouncements on theological points may have been occasionally complex but at the same time were always clear. Perhaps Pascal realized this about himself, and that was why he broke off in the middle of a sentence in the nineteenth *Provinciale.* Certainly, by now, the Jansenists had lost the theological war; and perhaps Pascal was trying to accommodate with the Jesuits, as he always accused them of doing. As modern critics argue, the Jesuits represented the *esprit de finesse,* and they had emphatically won over the Jansenist *esprit de géométric.* After the destruction of Port-Royal, Catholicism would not be further fragmented, possibly by a Gallican Church or a Dutch Church, as the Anglican Church had been fragmented and compartmentalized by the Protestant challenge and, in certain salient respects, even by Puritanism within that Protestant challenge.

As a religious philosopher, Pascal immediately tips his hand. He states that the Catholic Church must argue with the Calvinist as one equal to another. The Catholics must lay authority aside, since it is wrongly based on Thomistic scholasticism, and make "use of reason." In a word, Pascal is spiritually a Protestant who wishes emotionally to stay in contact with the

Catholic Church. Hence, Pascal's Apology and especially the *Pensées* are truly Protestant criticisms of an orthodox Catholic Christianity to which the critic, Pascal, still yet has keen emotional ties. The question now is, as Morris Bishop phrased it, whether the Apology may be reconstructed from the *Pensées*, and if so, whether it is even proper. Let us ignore the question for the purpose of our essay and proceed directly into a consideration of the *Pensées*.

What is Pascal trying to do? In a word, it is to ascribe meaning to existence—and in an essentialist sense at that, since Pascal is ever removed from existentialism. He is compelled to do this because he suffers from a consciousness of the dual nature of man, in his grandeur and with his misery. Man is a thinking reed, to be sure; and though he can be broken easily, he is yet superior to the cosmos that crushes him, precisely because he knows he is suffering, just as Epictetus (the *roseau pensant*) was superior to the sadistic man (*univers*) who broke his arm. This, to Pascal, is the essential problem for our Christian, i.e., our tragic hero, keenly conscious of his grandeur and misery, to resolve. Therefore, it is the chief subject of the *Pensées*—and, indeed, the one point of unity in all the rather disjointed and even chaotic aphorisms about the nature of man.

The weakness of the *Pensées*, from the religious standpoint, is painfully apparent. Like Immanuel Kant's *The Critique of Pure Reason,* the *Pensées* suffers from overabstraction. In a significant way, this may very well be an implicit attack on his old adversaries, the Jesuits. For their study of ethical principles to concrete cases called *casuistry*, upon which is based the whole sacrament of reconciliation in Catholic Christianity, was the target. Because of Pascal's vicious and vindictive attacks, explicit in *Les Lettres provinciales* and implicit in the *Pensées*, the very word *casuistry* has a pejorative connotation today. Yet, in itself, casuistry is a meritorious example of moral judgment; indeed, it is as old as the very consciousness of morality, and in a real sense it even antedates Catholic Christianity. Moreover, in casuistry, even non-Jesuits agreed that a confessor might invoke a minority opinion in the judgment of the morality of a particular case. This is called *probabilism,* which, with his anti-Jesuit bias and his pro-Calvinist sentiment, Pascal religiously eschewed.

To return to our initial comment, we find the *Pensées* weak in practical application to individual cases; and does not the concrete case always interest us before we consider the abstract principles applicable to that case? The *Pensées*, it seems to us, loses dynamic impact through a singular lack of emphasis on peculiarity and particularity. We do not criticize Pascal because, as Catholic critics, we feel that he was really a Calvinist in his innermost heart. Indeed, we greatly admire the atheistic Friedrich Nietzsche for *Thus Spake Zarathustra* and *Beyond Good and Evil,* also aphoristic books. But Nietsche is incredibly strong, while Pascal is unbelievably weak. In other words, Nietzsche's aphorisms are schematized and imply a synthesis that we can analyze, while regrettably Pascal is diffuse, often tedious, and more often still strained and laborious. Moreover, Nietzsche epitomized German prose poetry at its very apogee in these two immortal works, while Pascal is commonly recognized for a journalistic style in the *Pensées.* Is a paragraph from *Le Figaro* poetic? Even as Catholic critics, we might opt for the Communist *L'Humanité* when it concerns journalistic style.

Morris Bishop observes that poetry exists on two different levels in Pascal: the poetry of ideas and the poetry of private emotion. We find this a cogent observation about the substance of the *Pensées,* but we must dissent from Professor Bishop's rather curious view that the *Pensées* merits its place in the canon of great literature and great thought. The ideas, to our way of thinking, are not sufficiently schematized to be truly a poetry of ideas, as Nietzsche's poetry is always also high philosophy. However, we agree in a sense that the *Pensées* is a poetry of private emotion. But it is precisely on this point that we believe Pascal most obviously fails as a Christian—certainly, as a Catholic.

For while Protestants may regard worship as a private and individual concern, Catholics are inclined to corporate worship, as in the Eucharist, as the public and general affirmation of our private and individual prayers. Perhaps this is the most significant reason why we are Catholics and why we feel that Pascal was really a Calvinist writing incognito.

What, in summary, are we trying so desperately to say that will alienate the modern world?

It is simply, emphatically this. We are committed, but to a religious position; not to an aesthetic or even philosophical position; our Catholicism. Too, what most differentiates Catholicism and Protestantism for us is the obvious fact that Catholics interpret *caritas* (selfless love) and *koinonia* (Christian communist community) in a different way than do most Protestants, though we do not maintain there is a unity in their respective positions. By *caritas,* we include the duality of man in the need for carnival as well as for Lent, for the flesh as well as for the soul, though apparently Pascal, in the Puritan lineage of Calvinism, opted for eternal Lent and ever eschewed Mardi Gras. In a word, he did not understand the Christian nature of joy, as Paul Claudel always did. Do not even the angels sing for joy? Is heaven not a joyful place? The true saint is always beatifically happy, ever elated, even in martyrdom—indeed, especially by martyrdom. It is precisely this aspect of *caritas*, love as joy, that Pascal fails to apprehend in his rather dour, drab, and one-dimensional appreciation of Christianity, especially when he claims to be a Catholic, when Catholics traditionally love joy.

This, too, leads into *koinonia,* or Christian communistic community. The Catholic faith is universal, or properly catholic, and the Catholic Church is without question a vast *koinonia,* subdivided into many smaller *koinonias.* Yet the Protestant faith is atomistic, with its emphasis on the individual in *koinonia* and not truly in the relationship of the individual to *koinonia,* or the inclusive totality of the aggregate community. To this extent, it seems to us that Pascal, as a Protestant, errs spiritually by being more self-oriented, as in individual prayers, than the Catholic in his *koinonia* orientation of and by and through and in *caritas,* or in the selfless love and absorption of self into community through love, which dissolves the "thinginess' and existential viscosity of life in its existential despair and brings all us Christian believers together in a corporate worship where we lose consciousness of self, surely the true goal of the mystic who loses himself, not merely in Christ Crucified, but also and more significantly in Christ Reborn.

What do we now conclude? Regrettably, we feel that Blaise Pascal is the most overrated mind in Occidental history. We feel that he failed in all particulars as a man, as a literary figure, and as a Catholic. He might very well have been a great scientist if he had not lost himself in technocracy. It would be pleasant to remember him as a great scientist who may or may not have been a devoted Catholic, since that doesn't even concern us. As it is, we fear Pascal was the most tragic hero under consideration: because he was not the Catholic he pretended to be, even to himself, especially to himself, in a remarkable lack of insight through an absurb persona: and because the *deus absconditus* always eluded him, like the pot of gold at the end of a leprechaun's rainbow in Ireland, the present seat of Jansenism in the Catholic Communion, since Jansenism is apparently alive and doing well.

Racine as Christian Tragic Hero

Quite possibly, Jean Racine is, outside France, the most underrated great writer who ever lived. In English, particularly, we do not properly appreciate his great genius: the incomparable poetry, the incredible drama, the superb psychological analysis. In this essay, we shall consider Racine as he has rarely been studied before, that is, in his real dimensions as a Christian tragic hero, a subject that may be surprising since he dealt with classic and Jewish protagonists, and with the former with more understanding than the latter, since he apparently considered the Jews "a peculiar people." But just as surely as Shakespeare peopled antiquity with Elizabethan courtiers, Racine ever depicted Catholic and even Jansenist men and women in his Greek and Roman pagans and in his Jews. This, we believe, will afford new insight into this incomparable poet-dramatist, who has been overtaught but not overly understood in France and tragically undervalued outside France.

A good popular treatment, though somewhat banal, is Claude Abraham's *Jean Racine.* In French, an older study is still of some value, particularly from the biographical standpoint: Daniel Mornet's *Jean Racine.* Philip Butler admirably and even definitively situates him in time and space, in harmony with his *Zeitgeist*, with his *Classicisme et baroque dans l'oeuvre de Racine,* a remarkably rich study. For contemporary reaction, we signal A Bonzon's authoritative *La Nouvelle critique de Racine.* Of special value to us in this essay were Odette de Mourgues' *Racine or the Triumph of Relevance* and John C. Lapp's *Aspects of Racinian Tragedy.* But nobody, to our knowledge, has emphasized the peculiarly Christian character of Racine's tragic hero, since everyone has assumed that his men and women are pagans and Jews, while in sober fact they are all Catholics (and also Jansenists) in painfully transparent disguise, anachronistically relocated in space to Greece, Rome, and Palestine.

We shall not concern ourselves with Racine's two aesthetic failures, *La Thébaïde* and *Alexandre,* though they were enormous popular successes at the time and established Racine's enviable reputation. Nor shall we concern ourselves with his two Jewish tragedies, *Esther* and *Athalie,* which marked the decline of his poetic powers and which were not so "Christian," though admittedly "Jewish," as the pagan (and Stoical) plays. *Les Plaideurs,* of course, is a comedy, and thus is really foreign to Racine's tragic temperament and of no use to a study of the Christian tragic hero. We may also disqualify *Bérénice, Bajazet, Mithridate,* and *Iphigénie* as extra and perhaps superfluous observations upon the archetypal Christian hero. Thus, we are left with the three greatest tragedies, *Andromaque, Britannicus,* and *Phèdre,* surely among the glories of world literature. They interest us exclusively in our consideration of the archetype of the Christian tragic hero, which so clearly emerges despite the Roman togas among the classical alexandrines with their cadenced phrases.

First, let us consider *Andromaque,* the first of Racine's three immortal plays, for its poetic diction and psychological perception. It is the story of Troy, of its funeral pyre, of its smoke and ashes, of the men and women who suffered and lived and who lived because they had suffered. This is the great play upon which not only the fate of nations but also, and more importantly, the destiny of men and women (our heroes) are acted out.

Of course, his Greek chieftains are really French noblemen, and his pagans are Christian tragic heroes. Indeed, however, does it all matter? For that is precisely our point. There is an undeniable majesty and grandeur in the alexandrines, as if they were the very substance of the noblest Greek drama, too. The sentiment, the ambience, however, is pure Versailles, and that is why it was an instantaneous success when it was first produced—and one of the reasons it has survived.

The scene is set in Epirus, at the court of Pyrrhus, son of Achilles, a scant year after the fall of Troy. Among his captives of war are Andromaque, Hector's widow, and her infant son, Astyanax. Pyrrhus, deeply in love with her, is neglecting Hermione, his betrothed. The Greek kings are concerned. Consequently, they have sent an ambassador, Oreste, to obtain possession of Astyanax, so that Pyrrhus will regain his reason and reclaim his duty to his city-state. But Oreste falls in love with Hermione and hopes to fail in his mission, so that he may carry her back to his own native city-state.

All depends on Andromaque. If she surrenders herself to Pyrrhus, he will forsake Hermione, and Oreste will get Hermione. If Andromaque rejects Pyrrhus, he will return to his fiancée and surrender Astyanax to the Greeks, who fear in him a resurgence of Trojan power. Andromaque wavers, as destiny fluctuates upon her existential option. She makes up her mind to remain loyal to the memory of her beloved husband, Hector. If she can get Pyrrhus to swear to protect Astyanax, she will kill herself rather than surrender her body and being to her master. Hermione, in outrage, demands that Oreste avenge her honor. He agrees to this at the very altar where Pyrrhus pledges his faith to Andromaque, but it is too late. The Greeks kill Pyrrhus, as he admits he will marry Andromaque, since they fear Astyanax upon the Trojan throne. Oreste brings the news to Hermione, who ceases to hate Pyrrhus upon learning of his tragic death. Now she remembers her great love for him. In existential despair, consumed by nausea, she opts for death. She kills herself upon the body of Pyrrhus. Then Oreste loses his mind. In the dénouement, he is dragged off by the Greeks, who escape from an angry mob intent on avenging a dead king. This is, in summary, the sober action of the stark tragedy.

As a profoundly Christian drama, *Andromaque* turns upon the existential options, whether for good or for evil, of the protagonists, the Christian tragic heroes and heroines. The action turns upon an eventful crisis, a profoundly psychological crisis, in a once great queen. Too, it depicts a Rimbaldian *descente aux enfers* for a royal family, now fallen into moral ruin, existential despair, existential nausea, neurasthenia, abulia. Andromaque errs existentially when she opts, as circumstances force her to opt, for a course of action that betrays the *bonne foi* of her once noble past. She makes this choice in all the glaring absurdity of an existential *acte gratuit,* or gratuitous act, or meaningless act.

Pyrrhus is tragic, too, in his sadomasochism and his love-hate ambivalences and ambiguities, which obviate meaningful options in the existential sense within a somber world of despair, disgust, nausea. And is not all carnal love without Christian *caritas* (selflessness) in *koinonia* (Christian community) profoundly sadomasochistic in seemingly inextricable kinds of double-binds of emotional bondage, always in a slave-master relationship? Duty, for the head, always loses to the heart, or passion, particularly in the animus and anima of the Dark Heart of Man and Woman. As a hurt woman, Andromaque has a plan, and a good one, to save Astyanax and to preserve her chastity, as she seeks to enlist Hermione's aid to make Pyrrhus assent to her request, her demand. Yet Hermione is bent on revenge, and thus she opts absurdly and gratuitously for a personal evil and not the common good.

How does Andromaque intend to make her ultimate existential option? She determines to marry Pyrrhus to save her beloved son, but after the ceremony, after he has promised to protect Astyanax, she will commit suicide. Really, she knows that Pyrrhus is a violent man with a passionate heart, without principle, who will never keep his word after he realizes he has been tricked. Thus, in the existential sense, Andromaque is self-deceived; and such a person cannot opt meaningfully, as Andromaque purposes to do. Indeed, even the son she claims to love, ultimately, is but a mirror to her vanity, her very feminine vanity. In the end, Andromaque is as vain as she is stubborn, surely great Christian sins that Racine, consciously and also self-consciously, recognized as sins in Greece and at Versailles.

Yet Andromaque, in her blundering way, manages to survive. Is this, indeed, the natural consequence of her natural lucidity in a kind of Aristotelian golden mean? No, we think not. For the World, the Flesh, and the Devil, in the profound Christian presence of Versailles, is totally absurd: utterly meaningless. They know the differences between good and evil in the Christian and not Nietzschean sense, but they simply never opt for it. Passion triumphs, and passion is madness, and madness is existential absurdity, and absurdity is also evil in the Christian sense, since the Christian cosmos derives its metaphysical meaning in its relationship of the true believer in Christ, or the principle of selfless love.

Pyrrhus dies: tragically, of course, and quite pointlessly. Still, no one gets what he wants. Does the pagan ever? Does the Christian, ever? The Greeks kill Pyrrhus out of political necessity, itself far stronger than mere love or sadomasochistic passion. All human effort, in the end, is vain. In a Greek context, Racine, as a devout Jansenist, seems ever to have hedonistic Versailles at heart. All human effort, indeed, is absurd, quite meaningless, except in the total relationship to existential options within the cosmos of Christ for the Power, the Kingdom, and the Glory, ever antipodal to Satan (passion's) sadomasochistic Kingdom of the World, the Flesh, and the Devil.

What sort of pagan—i.e., Christian tragic hero, anachronistically transported in time and space—is Britannicus? Is he truly alone, isolated from *caritas* and *koinonia*, or does he have camaraderie in Narcisse, surely a symbolic name? Credulously, perhaps like most good Christians, themselves only simple and indeed almost simpleminded, he at first trusts Agrippine, only later to be bitterly disappointed, disabused, *déçu*. Like a good Aristotelian hero, Britannicus has a *hamartia* of *hubris*, or pride, just as, indeed, probably all Christian tragic heroes do.

Like a bad Christian, yet a Christian courtier at Versailles, he is extremely ambitious; and just as the Epicureans go in for *carpe diem,* so he openly voices his political ambitions. In the end, he is far too inexperienced in politics to realize that his posture only ensures his doom. In seeking to ameliorate his political situation, he only makes an absolute political necessity of his death. In the dénouement, he has his moment of truth and drops the faintest semblance of sham and hypocrisy, just as any true Christian eschews all sham and hypocrisy, because existentially it is *Schein* rather than *Sein.* Junie is his only chance of happiness, and in a theological sense she represents the Church just as he represents Christ, or Man, or Messiah, here to save a decadent pagan world from itself and for God. She is, as he thinks, his only real chance for genuine happiness; and that, indeed, is the motor force of his psychological and perhaps also spiritual tragedy. For Junie is only woman, therefore human, all too human; and this is, after all, a profane love. Man should ever choose, or strive to opt for, a higher, heavenly love.

Like all carnal love, Britannicus' passion for Junie is self-centered, imma-ture, even boyish. Certain critics have even marveled that the perspicacious Junie, surely the very incarnation of Goethe and Nietzsche's "das ewige Weibliche," could be so desperately immature and ingenuous. Still, is Junie always naïve? She doesnt' believe, either, any more than he, in sham, hypoc-risy, deception. Moreover, like a Christian tragic heroine, she is horrified by the decadent life at the imperial court, itself out of the World, the Flesh, and the Devil. Even late in the play, she is doomed by the dichotomy *Schein...- Sein,* or appearance...reality, or the discrepancy between word and deed, between *acte gratuit* and meaningful act. In the end, Néron manages to "pollute" her with the *faisandage* of his gamey court. In the end, merely in order to survive, she puts on her Jungian persona, as indeed she must, to meet the terrible reality of the World, the Flesh, and the Devil. Like all real women, too, she is profoundly maternal, especially in her care and concern for Britannicus, almost like a devoted mother for an ailing son.

There are no real idealists in *Britannicus,* as if, indeed, such a man could long survive in Rome or at Versailles. Even Burrhus, with whom we so openly sympathize, is an opportunist—indeed, an *arriviste.* Perhaps he is really self-deceived, even self-abused, not at all innocent, and certainly not ingenuous. Rome is Versailles, in a word, and a rose is a rose is a rose is a rose, as Gertrude Stein would so meaningfully say in a metaphysical sense. In the end, he cannot resist the evil Néron, himself the prototype of the Antichrist of the Apocalypse of the Book of *Revelation,* the very whore of Rome. In the end, too, he even seeks an alliance with Agrippine, who can no longer control her son, the insidious Néron, and rule though him. But while he pretends morality, she prattles of pure power; and there is no viable com-munication between them. What is Burrhus but a politician who cannot quite carry it off in Versailles, i.e., Rome? As in the World, the Flesh, the Devil—i.e., Rome Eternal, or Versailles—nobody can compromise in the very dimensions of his evil, and in the end everybody tragically opts for evil, not good, and ever, at that, in meaningless *actes gratuits.*

What we discover from the Roman court of the Emperor Néron is that, since there is no viable *caritas*, there can be no camaraderie; hence, too, there is no *koinonia.* In the play, only Agrippine has a confidante, not truly a friend, since without *caritas* there can be no camaraderie in a kind of *koinonia.* Ultimately, Agrippine is isolated even from the self-discovered Néron. Agrippine is an Epicurean, even a hedonist, as many Christians really are. She shows neither shame nor self-respect as she amorally confesses how she has sacrificed everything good, true, and noble in her lust for power. She murdered her own husband, not selflessly for her son, the cruel Néron, but rather so that she could govern selfishly through the mouthpiece of her son. In the end, she loses the faintest semblance of lucidity as an ideal of the Aristotelian golden mean. She is self-deluded, and in an existential sense this is the very measure and definition of metaphysical evil. Hence, indeed, deluded, she dies, for she must die because of, in, and through that very delusion: a failure to appreciate and apprehend moral reality.

In a Christian sense, the opposite of love, or *caritas*, or selflessness, is selfishness, possessiveness. Certainly, too, this selfishness defines and depicts Agrippine more than any other quality. She changes in the play, develops, metamorphoses, though Néron does not. From an evil adolescent, he matures with blinding speed into an evil adult. Yet Agrippine is brave, while Néron remains essentially a coward.

The pagans all lacked Christian humility, just as, indeed, in the World, the Flesh, and the Devil, all Christians lacked it, too, except for a handful of calendar saints. The vain Burrhus, therefore, appeals to Néron's vanity, essentially pagan, though also Christian in far more than simply *amour propre.* Too, the true sense is more than mere carnality. Hence, Néron's passion for Junie is not really sexual, since that could be understood and even forgiven. Political necessity ever controls him as a political monster, just as the murder of Britannicus was motivated by political aims. In this sense, the Christian saint is apolitical, ever concerned with the Kingdom, the Power, and the Glory, and not with the World, the Flesh, and the Devil of Rome Eternal, or, as it really is, Versailles. Moreover, Néron is into sadomasochism, while Christian love, or *caritas,* is selfless, object-oriented, and not at all self-oriented.

Néron's mother, Agrippine, however, is even more cunning and cruel than he—in that sense, more truly evil. Augustus, his idol, was a Stoic who could and did truly master himself; but Néron cannot control his own human emotions. In the end, his resolve to murder Agrippine is a blind and totally absurd *acte gratuit.* In acting against her, therefore, he also reacts against himself and the good instincts always inherent in everyone's angelic self.

Christianity, too, is a matter of masks, of Jungian personas, or, rather, of the hero's being honest with himself and with others and refusing to wear one. Pagans, and bad Christians, are all actors in the absurd drama of the World, the Flesh, and the Devil, and bad actors at that. It is a far too cerebral world for Stoicism, Epicureanism, hedonism, just as it is for Christian existentialism. In the end, within all the perverse *voyeurisme,* itself "le vice suprême," as if out of Joséphin Péladan's *La Décadence latine,* Rome, like Versailles, is too heavily cerebral. Abulia, or the inability to opt meaningfully in a context for good and evil, here Roman, yet also Christian at Versailles, is the ultimate sin against the Holy Ghost of Christian existentialist philosophy.

Thus, most meaningfully of all, Néron fails not only as dictator, as Caesar, but also, most regrettably, as a human being, trying to realize his existentialist possibilities. He is essentially impotent as the measure of the failure of the man, of the Christian tragic hero: of Man, too. Néron, on the surface of the action, triumphs, just as invariably the Christian tragic hero is overwhelmed by Satan in the cosmos of the World, the Flesh, and the Devil. He has superimposed his new order on Rome, and it is the gamey incarnation of a heady, all too cerebral evil, in the metaphysical dimensions of abulia. Junie triumphs, however, even in the evil context of Rome Eternal, or Versailles, as she manages to escape the metaphysical monster of Néron, or Satan, or Whore of Rome, the antipode to Christ, the Church, and the Kingdom, the Power, and the Glory. At a glance, it will be seen that in a surrealist sense *Britannicus* is Racine's most relevant play, for it truly speaks to us would-be Christians as we attempt to cope with our own social order, always evil by definition.

Phèdre is Racine's masterpiece, unquestionably one of the immortal works of world literature. At the same time, it is his simplest drama and also, structurally, though not aesthetically or psychologically, one of the simplest dramas of world literature. In this context, we are all familiar with the Greek legend, especially as it appears in Euripides' famous work of that name. But the cardinal point is that Racine made certain striking changes to effect his own purpose, and this is what we want to stress now in our recounting of his familiar plot.

Thésée, King of Athens, an old man with a young wife and a younger son, has been gone from Athens for six months. His dutiful son, Hippolyte, is concerned for his father's safety and by his own consuming love for Aricie, daughter and last member of a family of powerful political adversaries exterminated by Thésée. With this in mind, the king has even forbidden her to marry, for he wants to liquidate that family line. Moreover, Hippolyte is perturbed by the apparent hatred of his beautiful young stepmother, Phèdre, scarcely older than he. Phèdre, erroneously enough, thinks she is dying, though we doubt that anyone ever died of a broken heart. In this fatal mood, she tells Oenone, her devoted nurse and confidante, that she is so cruel to Hippolyte because she wishes to hide her love from him—and, indeed, even from herself.

Then the rumor circulates that Thésée is dead. Joyfully, following Oenone's suggestion, Phèdre confesses her fatal passion to Hippolyte, though he himself loves Aricie. Rather curtly, even cruelly, Hippolyte rejects his stepmother's advances. Then Thésée, very much alive, appears. Frightened by the possibility the awful truth might come out, Phèdre permits Oenone, her dear friend, to slander Hippolyte, even to accuse him of trying to seduce her. Then Phèdre discovers that Hippolyte loves Aricie totally, and in a fit of guilt, jealousy, she once more turns to Oenone for advice and consolation. For his part, Thésée misconstrues his son's silence and banishes him from the palace, cursing him, calling upon the sea god Neptune to avenge his outraged honor. In the end, Neptune, as if with the Minotaur, whom Thésée had slain in the Cretan labyrinth, sends a monster who stamps on Hippolyte's horses and then drags the tragic hero to his death. Later, Phèdre, in a fit of remorse, poisons herself and then tells Thésée the truth. With her last words, she clears the lover whose embraces she never enjoyed.

This simple plot is beautifully cadenced and balanced. Hippolyte tells of his love for Aricie to his confidante, Théramène, while Phèdre reveals her fatal passion to her own confidante, Oenone. Likewise, each act is beautifully structured and balanced with classic theses and antitheses. There are two love affairs. Moreover, as the French rightly say, "la tragédie de l'amour, c'est qu'on aime quand on n'est pas aimé, et on n'aime pas quand on est aimé." As if in the Aldous Huxley novel, *Phèdre*, the great neoclassic drama in France, is all too much a matter of beautifully structured, arranged, and cadenced "point-counterpoint."

The tragedy is one of loneliness, of the Christian isolation of the soul and the human heart, since passion is not *caritas* and does not lead into *koinonia* but into a selfish desire, even a lust, that in its carnality keeps the human breast from existentially opting for God. In this sober, somber, stark solitude of *Phèdre,* within its poetic magnificence, perhaps the noblest play written since Periclean Greece, the tragedy is one of wrong options. Everybody, in a word, seems to make the wrong options for the right reasons—or, rather, the wrong reasons. This is how, almost mathematically, as if following a geometric equation, the protagonists, the Christian tragic heroes and heroines, bring upon themselves their tragic destiny, as if superimposed upon them by the Greek Wyrd, the abstract power as Destiny that is greater than the gods.

Sadomasochism is a leitmotif in the unknotting of this most classical of modern tragedies. All motives are dichotomies. Phèdre, as the daughter of Minos, is "wisdom," for Minos means "wisdom." At the same time, she is also lust, for her mother's name, Pasiphaë, signifies lust. She is knotted to the past, and almost hesitantly she anticipates the future with a full-blown Greek sense of ultimate doom and disaster in her existential despair. She is morally aware of herself and her carnal limitations. Yet, enigmatically and problematically, she is aware of her immorality, that is, if immorality can be construed as the acute consciousness of immorality. Always, too, Phèdre loses herself, masochistically taking delight in the suffering (*la souffrance*) that she experiences through her incestuous passion for Hippolyte, her handsome stepson.

She is a woman, at least a young woman, though not a matron; and apparently she is not overly skilled or much practiced in the delicate Grecian arts of love. She does not ever pretend to set a trap for Hippolyte when she attempts to seduce him; rather, she makes a honest declaration of her love, itself a fatal incestuous passion. She criticizes herself. She feels she is immoral. She hates herself for her immorality. Still, her rabid self-accusation—quite sadomasochistic in itself, by the way—has its proper dimension of overt sexuality, which she enjoys through its keen and cutting pain. It is love. It is death. It is love-death that she feels, that she suffers, that delights her through its mystical and almost surrealistic suffering, *la souffrance.*

In Euripides, Hippolyte was rather bovinely and one-dimensionally proud of his chastity. In Racine, he rues it; yet he does not really miss it and is, in a psychological sense, a veritable slave to Venus through his fatal passion for Aricie. He bemoans love, yet he delights in Aricie's love and recoils from Phèdre's incestuous love. Yet, really, *Phèdre* is a psychological study only in neoclassic terms. In the more detailed and lurid terms of contemporary psychiatry, Phèdre and Hippolyte are almost one-dimensional in substance and texture. They merely waver. They do not change. They do not develop. Indeed, they are stasis within the kinesis of what is an existential document, and this causes a peculiar dynamic inner tension in us, giving us an aesthetic delight and psychological understanding of the nature of tragedy.

Clearly, Phèdre is the heroine, our Christian tragic heroine, consumed by guilt and shame for her carnal love, itself also incestuous. Racine's greatest characterizations tend to be women more often than men. Racine had a feminine soul, like Alfred de Musset, which enabled him to emphathize with women far more than most men can, with their different sensibilities, values, frames of reference. Hippolyte opts for Aricie, who opts for family honor and political reconciliation perhaps more than she opts for Hippolyte, himself a symbol of political rapprochement with Thésée as much as a flesh-and-blood man. Phèdre opts for Hippolyte, who chastely opts for an etherealized, spiritual love rather than for a fatal incestuous carnality. Oenone opts for Phèdre, while Théramène opts for Hippolyte; and both confidants, we fear, opt evilly and act evilly upon our Christian heroes with their wrong existential options. In atheistic existentialism, as with Jean-Paul Sartre and Martin Heidegger, the important consideration is simply to act meaningfully and then to accept responsibility for that action in *bonne foi,* but in Christian existentialism our tragic hero (and existentialism is essentially a tragic philosophy) is to opt meaningfully for good and not for evil in God's Christian cosmos.

Ironically, just as sadomasochism motivates all our heroes and heroines— indeed, all our protagonists in a kind of slave-master relationship—so, too, the trouble comes from "sexual purity," or Puritanism, divorced from the breadth of Catholic essentialism. Are we really surprised to discover that our Christian tragic heroes and heroines are indeed Puritans within a Catholic context, as if they had heretically stepped out of their simple cells at Port-Royal? They are just that, you know.

This purity, problematically enough, is the substance of "le mal," the evil, the passion from which our heroes and heroines suffer. "Le mal," indeed, is passion, one that our protagonists cannot cope with because none of them, including the rather innocent and ingenuous Phèdre, can really accept their carnal nature, though we assume that any classical pagan who frequented the hetairas in their bordellos could readily do so.

It is all a question of light and dark, of Ormazd and Ahriman, as if from the Zarathustrianism in which Christianity has certain roots, e.g., the concept of the resurrection of the dead. Light-dark, sadism-masochism, love-passion, time-timelessness, love-hate, words-meaning, stasis-kinesis—all of these antipodes are deliciously present in Jean Racine, himself the very hero, with his feminine and ever perversely Jansenist heart, and also heroine, both male and female, whom he ever portrayed in the *dramatis personae* of his most remarkable and singular protagonists. In the end, too, the Christian tragedy, in Christian dimensions, is that the Christian tragic hero, is overwhelmed by his "passion," if not his "orgueil" in that passion. In the incredible "movement" and "gestures" and "eye movements" of *Phèdre*, this, then, is the constant, the very index of the *passion* in the Christian sense. The movement of the eyes, interestingly enough, is also the index to that fatal "passion," which ever undoes the Christian sensibility and sensitivity. This is all one-dimensional, yes, and we certainly admit it. Emphatically, however, this one-dimensional psychology, almost a stereotype of neoclassic simplicity and bluntness, as it were, results in the most sophisticated study of dramatic soul-states ever known to the sublest court audience of all time, not excluding imperial Byzantium, that of Versailles in the existential moments of Louis XIV, the sun-king, in whom his court basked and for whom he radiated "comme le soleil."

What may we conclude, then, from our composite picture of Jean Racine? As commonly supposed, he was a Jansenist, that is, a Puritan within the Catholic Communion, reared and conditioned at Port-Royal: This is a salient point that we readily admit. At the same time, Racine was, we submit, truly a Catholic existentialist in the antipodal position of the Jesuits and their casuistry. For what, indeed, is Racine's dramaturgy but a study of casuistry, the specific case, divorced from its universal applications to man, woman, and all mankind? If Jansenism was stasis, and Racine were static, then Jesuitism was kinesis, and Racine was remarkably kinetic, too. Is this, then, not why we remember Racine as a man who was truly at least the equal of Dante and Shakespeare in his more circumscribed but also less romantic and therefore more universal and classical dimensions? It is the exquisite dynamic tension born of the rather Zen Buddhist reconciliation of aesthetic and emotional opposites in a kind of neoclassic totality and harmony in the proper Greek sense of that singular word.

This was classicism. This was Jean Racine. This was he at his best in his greatest masterpiece, *Phèdre,* as the Latins see it but as the Nordics and Anglo-Saxons regrettably do not. Too, this was the very definition of Racine's protagonists and of himself, too, as a composite, in his peculiar and particular configuration of the Christian tragic hero, a Protestant and even a Puritan as a Jansenist from Port-Royal searching desperately, rather desperately, always most desperately, for the pure illumination of the essential and existential Catholic faith represented in the Jesuit casuistry, which, in a remarkable breakdown of self-perception, he formally opposed to the bitter and embittered end.

Baudelaire as Christian Tragic Hero

It is tempting to generalize on the problem of Baudelaire as a Christian at all, much less as a Christian tragic hero; and to do so, of course, is to miss the pregnant point.

After the publication of Baudelaire's *Les Fleurs du mal* in 1857, the popular critics of the day hastened to point out the painfully apparent diabolical elements in him and dismissed him as a *sataniste farouche du bas-romantisme français.* Manifestly, this was never true even of Barbey d'Aurevilly, later, in the oblique lineage of Baudelaire. Still, in our own time, certain critics, most notable among them François Mauriac and Charles du Bos, both of them orthodox Roman Catholics, err most grievously when they all but term him *Saint Charles*, a worthy subject for canonization if he had only performed his two verifiable miracles. Shades of the simplistic and incredibly naïve Jean-Paul Sartre and Simone de Beauvoir, when they talk about Saint Jean Genêt and Saint Sade!

The problem, in a certain measure, reflects the failing of Aristotelian logic, which separates such weighty problems with *either...or* antitheses, leading to existential options of "good" and "evil." Far more sophisticated, we think, is the wisdom of the Orient, which assesses totality in terms of *both...and,* as the critics of Zen Buddhism like Alan Watts have so cogently pointed out, in the resolution of opposites. For opposites must be reconciled and incorporated in a spectrum of literary sensibility with its concomitant philosophical ramifications. Or, as the depth therapists would say as one school of modern psychiatry, Baudelaire is (is not) a saint sinner divine fool who ascends descends to heaven hell through his success failures as a poet nonperson. Such a statement, typical of double-bind depth therapy, is not just "cutesy" or even problematic. According to the wisdom of the East, it simply denotatively includes the *both...and* aspects of a most complicated poet and mystic, whom we shall now discuss as a Christian tragic hero, himself the autobiographical hero of all of his work, even solipsistically his own hero in his pungent and often acerbic art criticism.

What, then, is the problem? In his *Poetics,* Aristotle, who may very well have been wrong on this as well as on the *either...or* mode of critical analysis, states that a tragic hero is a great and august figure overwhelmed by his *hamartia,* or tragic flaw, with the result that in catharsis (the psychological purging of our emotions of pity and fear) we feel a real détente along with our understanding at the fall of the noble man. To be exact, he discusses this rather quaint and quite possibly fallacious theory, which literary history has lamentably apotheosized, in terms of Sophocles' *Oedipus the King.* Ever since that time, Aristotelian critics have waxed verbose and sometimes lachrymose as they espy *hamartias,* conveniently enough, behind every bramblebush in Western literature. While Aristotle had his cogent point to make, it is not at all demonstrable that even all of classical drama can properly be understood in terms of *hamartia* and *catharsis.* And as David Daiches Raphael points out in his excellent *Paradox of Tragedy*, the *hamartia* theory has never really applied in the case of the Christian tragic hero. For while forces in a social ethos may very well overwhelm the Christian hero, it is only his immortal soul that really counts, and never the corporeal envelope that tragically contains that immortal soul, the gift of God, the boon of heaven.

In this light, let us now consider Charles Baudelaire as a Christian tragic hero, for we readily admit that he was a Christian in the Catholic tradition. What, in a word, is tragedy for a Christian protagonist, that is, a Christian hero, in this case even a Catholic hero, as Baudelaire admittedly and also self-consciously is? There are several dimensions to this resolution (in the metaphysical sense), which include the hero's relationship to nature, the morality of the hero as a man and also as an artist, his consciousness and also even his self-consciousness of the psychological reality of sin, the divided self or ego, the meaning of freedom (in which existential options can meaningfully take place), and the Christian concept of time—or, as the Mormons would say, of Time and all Eternity—the theater upon which man acts to make those existential options to resolve his state of doubt and thus to achieve the Christian state of grace that leads ultimately and inevitably and also even inexorably to salvation.

The wary Baudelairean may wonder why we write at all of the Christian tragic hero in Baudelaire. For he recollects that in 1961 D.J. Mossop published *Baudelaire's Tragic Hero,* significantly subtitled, "A Study of the Architecture of *Les Fleurs du Mal.*" Moreover, this study is precisely what the subtitle indicates: a rather discursive and never schematic peregrination of the "poet-hero" (not the Christian tragic hero, as we believe) through the various poems of the individual sections of *Les Fleurs du mal*. Moreover, Professor Mossop does not plunge into the totality of the Christian and specifically Catholic experience when he waxes eloquent upon the worn motif of Baudelaire's sadomasochism. While this book is admittedly valuable to Baudelaireans, the title is somewhat misleading because Professor Massop always writes of the "poet-hero" and rarely delves in the "gouffre" of the philosophical, religious, and mystical elements of Baudelaire himself as his own Christian tragic hero.

Perhaps nobody who subscribes to the theory of "art for art's sake" (properly deriving from Théophile Gautier) can truly be a Christian. Certainly, this was the fundamental position implied in Baudelaire, for the Catholic has traditionally accepted nature and indeed based his Catholicism upon nature, containing both Apollonian elements of the divine and Dionysian elements of the demonic. Catholicism was never a simplistic faith in which nature was altogether bad, especially since it was supposedly "not beautiful" to the poet, decadent perhaps for that reason. In particular, Baudelaire denies an integral part of his Catholic heritage of wholeness and totality as the poet of the city, totally divorced from nature, when he fragmentizes, so to speak, the concept of nature.

Now, Baudelaire's diatribes against nature, as best expressed in his exemplary essay "Du Maquillage," and by extension his objections to sanity or wholeness or totality, have often been noted. Let us cite a single example, "Les Bijoux," in itself instructive, since it concerns the mulatto Jeanne Duval, herself the great passion and perhaps abiding love of Baudelaire's life:

> La très chère était nue, et, connaissant mon coeur,
> Elle n'avait gardé que ses bijoux sonores,
> Dont le riche attirail lui donnait l'air vainqueur
> Qu'ont dans leurs jours heureux les esclaves des Maures.
>
> Quand il jette en dansant son bruit vif et moqueur,
> Ce monde rayonnant de métal et de pierre
> Me ravit en extase, et j'aime à la fureur
> Les choses où le son se mêle à la lumière....
>
> —Et la lampe s'étant résignée à mourir,

> *Comme le foyer seul illuminait la chambre,*
> *Chaque fois qu'il poussait un flamboyant soupir,*
> *Il inondait de sang cette peau couleur d'ambre!*

What do we clearly see from these lines? As with Des Essentes in Huysmans' archetypal study of the French decadent, *A Rebours,* himself the decadent hero as well (and to this extent) as Christian tragic hero, Baudelaire was titillated exquisitely most by the artfulness of the jewels, far more than by his bien-aimée's beloved black body. What does this mean? Is titillation an abiding love, which predicates a connection with nature and not merely with art? We think not, as Baudelaire admitted in his cult of spleen and lassitude, most often a moral lassitude and indeed a moral surrender to spleen in abulia and neurasthenia. What does this mean, then, for Baudelaire's psyche? Clearly, it indicates a divorce from the Catholic tradition of wholeness and totality and love (Catholicity), in nature, through nature. To the extent that Baudelaire is aware of the irreconcilable tension within his immortal soul, he is in existential anguish and despair, consumed by an alienation from the wholeness and totality of nature: indeed, from love, since we feel strongly that love is in nature, or is perhaps nature itself, or is certainly caught up by natural process in *l'évolution créatrice.*

This leads into Baudelaire's Catholic morality, both as a man and as an artist. As a man, he accepts, or claims to accept, Catholic orthodoxy; and thus he is horrified, or pretends to be horrified, by his debauches. As an artist, however, he professes a credo of art divorced from nature, exemplified and even idealized in "l'art pour l'art," which would welcome, and does in fact welcome, adornment, titillation, and, ultimately, the debauch as the cerebral hero's supreme *raffinement.* To Baudelaire, then, was the artist not truly a vagabond gypsy, as in "Bohémiens en voyage":

> *La tribu prophétique aux prunelles ardentes*
> *Hier s'est mise en route, emportant ses petits*
> *Sur son dos, ou livrant à leurs fiers appétits*
> *Le trésor toujours prêt des mamelles pendantes.*
>
> *Les hommes vont à pied sous leurs armes luisantes*
> *Le long des chariots où les leurs sont blottis,*
> *Promenant sur le ciel des yeux appesantis*
> *Par le morne regret des chimères absentes.*
>
> *Du fond de son réduit sablonneux, le grillon,*

Les regardant passer, redouble sa chanson;
Cybèle, qui les aime, augmente ses verdures,

Fait couler le rocher et fleurir le désert
Devant ces voyageurs, pour lesquels est ouvert
L'empire familier des ténèbres futures.

The parallel is instructive. Hugo's "mage" and Vigny's "Moise" have become metamorphosed, in Baudelaire's mind, to the vagabond gypsy, himself a prototype of the poet, *vates,* seer, "le déshérité du monde maudit." Is this the cryptic vision of St. John the Divine in his Book of *Revelation*, the sort of hallucinatory writing of a true saint? Obviously not! Once again, therefore, Baudelaire, as a tragic Christian hero, reveals his almost schizophrenic divorce from nature (the land, or home), since the gypsy is indeed landless and homeless, and also his divorce from love (for that, too, entails land, home, togetherness, belonging), and thereby his divorce from the emotional and psychological stability to two thousand years of Catholic Christianity.

It is well-documented that Baudelaire believed in original sin, and, Calvinistically, at least at times, he seems to have believed in total depravity. Never, to our mind, was his Satanic pride more movingly portrayed, even in the far more famous "Les Litanies de Satan," than in "Châtiment de l'orgueil," where he describes the horrible reality of the consciousness (and also painful self-consciousness) of sin:

En ces temps merveilleux où la Théologie
Fleurit avec le plus de sève et d'énergie,
On raconte qu'un jour un docteur des plus grands,
—Après avoir forcé les coeurs indifférents;
Les avoir remués dans leurs profondeurs noires;
Après avoir franchi vers les célestes gloires
Des chemins singuliers à lui-même inconnus,
Où les purs Esprits seuls peut-être étaient venus,--
Comme un homme monté trop haut, pris de panique,
S'écria, transporté d'un orgueil satanique:
"Jésus, petit Jésus! je t'ai poussé bien haut!
Mais, si j'avais voulu t'attaquer au défaut
De l'armure, ta honte égalerait ta gloire,
Et tu ne serais plus qu'un foetus dérisoire!"

Immédiatement sa raison s'en alla.
L'éclat de ce soleil d'un crêpe se voila;
Tout le chaos roula dans cette intelligence,
Temple autrefois vivant, plein d'ordre et d'opulence,
Sous les plafonds duquel tant de pompe avait lui.
Le silence et la nuit s'installèrent en lui,
Comme dans un caveau dont la clef est perdue.
Dès lors il fut semblable aux bêtes de la rue,
Et, quand il s'en allait sans rien voir, à travers
Les champs, sans distinguer les étés des hivers,
Sale, inutile et laid comme une chose usée,
Il faisait des enfants la joie et la risée.

In other words, the reality of sin (in the Catholic world view, always Satanic pride, not sensual excess) is such that it is a mockery to man and God—and, indeed, a kind of madness, because it breaks the great chain of being when man, mere man, halfway between God and animal life, tries, vainly and vaingloriously of course, to usurp God's place as the head and chief link of that chain of being.

Since there is no wholeness (therefore, no sanity) in Baudelaire, since the totality of his Catholic world view has been fragmented by sin (Satanic pride), his self, or ego, is thereby divided and compartmentalized, as the familiar *homo duplex,* emerging in *bas-romantisme* and triumphant *décadence littéraire.* The concluding quatrains from "L'Héauton-timorouménos" are instructive in this regard:

Ne suis-je pas un faux accord
Dans la divine symphonie,
Grâce à la vorace Ironie
Qui me secoue et qui me mord?

Elle est dans ma voie, la criarde!
C'est tout mon sang, ce poison noir!
Je suis le sinistre miroir
Où la mégère se regarde!

Je suis la plaie et le couteau!
Je suis le soufflet et la joue!
Je suis les membres et la roue,
Et la victime et le bourreau!

Je suis de mon coeur le vampire,
—Un de ces grands abandonnés
Au rire éternel condamnés,
Et qui ne peuvent plus sourire!

In a Catholic sense, perhaps, Baudelaire as sinner (flesh) is the victim of himself as saint (soul); and this is his true dimension as the *homo duplex.* Yet, is it not also curious that the saint (soul) should be executioner? Here, clearly, Baudelaire speaks as an artist, a true bohemian, *un décadent des décadents,* railing out against the Catholicism that he professes but simultaneously finds uncomfortable and even offensive. The *homo duplex,* therefore, is a kind of schizophrenic hero, quite compartmentalized, unable to reform (reconstitute) his warring selves, as Saint Augustine did as sinner (in the flesh) and saint (in the spirit). At this point, the tension in Baudelaire as a tragic hero becomes absolutely unbearable, for in a psychological sense he cannot coordinate his "affect" into the meaningful actions of Catholic options, themselves truly existentialist in nature and kind.

What, to Baudelaire, is the meaning of freedom, which Catholics like to talk about? In a word, there is none. Baudelaire inhabits a closed, not an open, universe, where an uncertainty principle is at play, affording the hero viable existential options. In this sense, "Spleen IV" has not received the notice it deserves as a portrait of the Christian tragic hero paralyzed by abulia by a world that always crushes him and obviates his existential options:

Quand le ciel bas et lourd pèse comme un couvercle
Sur l'esprit gémissant en proie aux longs ennuis,
Et que de l'horizon embrassant tout le cercle
Il nous verse un jour noir plus triste que les nuits;

Quand la terre est changée en un cachot humide,
Où l'Espérance, comme une chauve-souris,
S'en va battant les murs de son aile timide
Et se cognant la tête à des plafonds pourris;

Quand la pluie étalant ses immenses traînées
D'une vaste prison imite les barreaux,
Et qu'un peuple muet d'infâmes araignées
Vient tendre ses filets au fond de nos cerveaux,

Des cloches tout à coup sautent avec furie
Et lancent vers le ciel un affreux hurlement,
Ainsi que des esprits errants et sans patrie
Qui se mettent à geindre opiniâtrement.

—Et de longs corbillards, sans tambours ni musique,
Défilent lentement dans mon âme; l'Espoir,
Vaincu, pleure, et l'Angoisse atroce, despotique,
Sur mon crâne incliné plante son drapeau noir.

For does the saint in man not live by hope, "l'Espérance"? But as Baudelaire clearly states, as a Catholic, he feels such a keen despair, today an existential despair, with its concomitant existential nausea, that he can no longer act or make those meaningful choices that Christianity demands of the pilgrim on his way through the world to salvation. Instead, Baudelaire is a tragic hero because of the demonic self ("le dégoût," or that which motivates and entails "le dégoût") paralyzes the angelic self in the *homo duplex.* Thus, it is easy to see why Jean-Paul Sartre, as a critic, has interested himself so much in Baudelaire—namely, because of the existential despair and existential nausea and consciousness of a thinginess (earth as a moldy dungeon) from which the Christian tragic hero can never hope to extricate himself.

In Baudelaire, time is, as Georges Poulet intimates in his *Etudes sur le temps humain,* only the perception of time. This touches upon the impressionism that was to become so strong after Baudelaire in Rimbaud and Lautréamont and that was to become a literary period in Europe after the Grande Guerre. Nowhere is this impressionism more visible and viable than in "Les Métamorphoses du vampire," which has been understood far too often as a perhaps unfortunate example of Baudelaire's *bas-romantisme*— and, indeed, decadence:

La femme cependant, de sa bouche de fraise,
En se tordant ainsi qu'un serpent sur la braise,
Et pétrissant ses seins sur le fer de son busc,
Laissait couler ces mots tout imprégnés de musc:
—"Moi, j'ai la lèvre humide, et je sais la science
De perdre au fond d'un lit l'antique conscience.
Je sèche tous les pleurs sur mes seins triomphants,
Et fais rire les vieux du rire des enfants.
Je remplace, pour qui me voit nue et sans voiles,

La lune, le soleil, le ciel et les étoiles!
Je suis, mon cher savant, si docte aux voluptés,
Lorsque j'étouffe un homme en mes bras redoutés,
Ou lorsque j'abandonne aux morsures mon buste,
Timide et libertine, et fragile et robuste,
Que sur ces matelas qui se pâment d'émoi,
Les anges impuissants se damneraient pour moi!"

Quand elle eut de mes os sucé toute la moelle,
Et que languissamment je me tournai vers elle
Pour lui rendre un baiser d'amour, je ne vis plus
Qu'une outre aux flancs gluants, toute pleine de pus!
Je fermai les deux yeux, dans ma froide épouvante,
Et quand je les rouvris à la clarté vivante,
A mes côtés, au lieu du mannequin puissant
Qui semblait avoir fait provision de sang,
Tremblaient confusément des débris de squelette,
Qui d'eux-mêmes rendaient le cri d'une girouette
Ou d'une enseigne, au bout d'une tringle de fer,
Que balance le vent pendant les nuits d'hiver.

It is the peculiar Christian consciousness of time that interests us in this highly impressionistic poem. For time, to the Christian, is not mere fact, event, actuality, or the mechanical ticking away of instants. It is not merely a shifting sense-impression temporally perceived, either, in what Arthur Rimbaud might well call "le dérèglement de tous les sens." Rather, time is acute consciousness of fact, event, actuality, with a Christian understanding of fact, event, actuality, and a Christian movement because of it, as when Baudelaire realizes (in that eternal moment of time, making his Kierkegaardian "saut dans l'éternité") that his beautiful beloved has spiritually been metamorphosed into a bloodsucking vampire. Time, then, for the Christian, is merely meaningful response to fact, event, actuality. Here, as elsewhere in *Les Fleurs du mal,* itself a kind of long confession in a hushed whisper to priest and reader, Baudelaire responds to time as a Christian tragic hero, as it weighs spiritually upon him, crushes his free will, damns him in despair and nausea, just as he preternaturally and clairvoyantly already knows he will be one day ineluctably damned.

Why is Baudelaire's peculiar understanding of time impressionistic—or, so to speak, solipsistic, perhaps indicating a confusion or disorientation in his mind-soul? In a word, it is his habitual state of doubt, his fundamental role as the proverbial "Doubting Thomas," for almost all contemporary criticism has erred by making a convinced and confirmed Catholic saint (a sadomasochist at that) of Baudelaire. Personally, we doubt that he ever enjoyed a moment of true belief, just as some Catholic priests merely go through the ritual of the Mass without conviction. Thus, in existential terms, Baudelaire could never make his *engagement.* Consequently, his acts were *actes gratuits* in vice and debauchery rather than existential options that took him turn by turn to "la Porte étroite": heaven.

Baudelaire's most exemplary poem on this salient point of his psychology is "Le Reniement de Saint Pierre," where he identifies totally with Saint Peter, who, though inconstant, yet was the "rock" upon which the Catholic Church was built:

> *Qu'est-ce que Dieu fait donc de ce flot d'anathèmes*
> *Qui monte tous les jours vers ses chers Séraphins?*
> *Comme un tyran gorgé de viande et de vins,*
> *Il s'endort au doux bruit de nos affreux blasphèmes.*
>
> *Les sanglots des martyrs et des suppliciés*
> *Sont une symphonie enivrante sans doute,*
> *Puisque, malgré le sang que leur volupté coûte,*
> *Les cieux ne s'en sont point encore rassasiés!*
>
> *—Ah! Jésus, souviens-toi du Jardin des Olives!*
> *Dans ta simplicité priais à genoux*
> *Celui qui dans son ciel riait au bruit des clous*
> *Que d'ignobles bourreaux plantaient dans tes chairs vives,*
>
> *Lorsque tu vis cracher sur ta divinité*
> *La crapule du corps de garde et des cuisines,*
> *Et lorsque tu sentis s'enfoncer les épines*
> *Dans ton crâne où vivait l'immense Humanité;*
>
> *Quand de ton corps brisé la pesanteur horrible*
> *Allongeait tes deux bras distendus, que ton sang*
> *Et ta sueur coulaient de ton front pâlissant,*
> *Quand tu fus devant tous posé comme une cible,*
>
> *Rêvais-tu de ces jours si brillants et si beaux*
> *Où tu vins pour remplir l'éternelle promesse,*

Où tu foulais, monté sur une douce ânesse,
Des chemins tout jonchés de fleurs et de rameaux,

Où, le coeur tout gonflé d'espoir et de vaillance,
Tu fouettais tous ces vils marchands à tour de bras,
Où tu fus maître enfin? Le remords n'a-t-il pas
Pénétré dans ton flanc plus avant que la lance?

—Certes, je sortirai, quant à moi, satisfait
D'un monde où l'action n'est pas la soeur du rêve;
Puissé-je user du glaive et périr par le glaive!
Saint Pierre a renié Jésus ... Il a bien fait!

Clearly, the saint, at least the calendar saint who can perform miracles through his mystical faith, has no doubts, for otherwise he would lack the psychic powers with which to perform those miracles. In contemporary existentialist literature, which we maintain Baudelaire was the great French writer of the nineteenth century to foreshadow, man doubts his own integrity, too, vis-à-vis the thinginess of a hostile or, at best, unfeeling world. The spleen of Baudelaire as well as his decadent lassitude and neurasthenia ends in existential despair and nausea. And why, really? Because Baudelaire, like Satan, aspires to be God, just as Saint Peter could never reach the perfection of the Messiah—and thus, sensing his own worthiness, in his fear, in his jealousy, betrayed the Messiah. Or, in more poetic terms, Baudelaire, as a Christian tragic hero, ever yearns for the "idéal" that, with his *bestial* nature, he can never hope to achieve. The result is abulia, the total paralysis of the will.

Yet, without ever saying as much, and thus perhaps without indulging in Pascal's religious vulgarity, Baudelaire, as his own tragic hero, does make his "pari," his wager, and thus makes his existential option for salvation. Momentarily, at least, he enjoys a state of grace that is only partly spiritual. Now, in stark truth, there are no great religious poems of faith, of total conviction, in *Les Fleurs du mal*. There are only fleeting moments, passing images, babbled words, as if in a troubled sleep or an ecstatic delirium of wine and opium. Doubt is always there: doubt, yes: and thus the existential anguish and nausea, with their debilitating abulia. Peculiarly enough, Baudelaire feels a "state of grace" only in art and love, as he writes in the liltingly beautiful "La Rançon":

L'homme a, pour payer sa rançon,

Deux champs au tuf profond et riche,
Qu'il faut qu'il remue et défriche
Avec le fer de la raison;

Pour obtenir la moindre rose,
Pour extorquer quelques épis,
Des pleurs salés de son front gris
Sans cesse il faut qu'il les arrose.

L'un est L'art, et l'autre l'Amour.
—Pour rendre le juge propice,
Lorsque de la stricte justice
Paraîtra le terrible jour.

Il faudra lui montrer des granges
Pleines de moissons, et des fleurs
Dont les formes et les couleurs
Gagnent le suffrage des Anges.

In this pregnant little poem, Baudelaire seems to subscribe to a kind of salvation by works through his state of spiritual grace—or "artistic inspiration," as it really is for him. Clearly, his focus is ever on art, i.e., poetry, in a rather desperate effort to achieve the "ideal," which otherwise eludes him: because he is not spiritual: because, in truth, as a *catholique manqué*, he has no real belief in heaven. Baudelaire is no *dévot;* he never was, except in the minds of the Roman Catholic critics like François Mauriac and Charles du Bos and an Anglo-Catholic commentator like T.S. Eliot. To be sure, Baudelaire is familiar, perhaps all to painfully familiar, with Christian trappings, concepts, ideas, forms, ritual, ceremonial—all of it hollow and empty. Unlike Prometheus, he does not believe with total conviction, and certainty thus does not breathe Christian fire in his works. At his best, he certainly foreshadows the Catholic existentialism of the twentieth century. Yet, too, he prefigures it in a negative way, dwelling almost exclusively (with his "fleurs maladives") upon despair and nausea, which make all existential options quite meaningless, futile, and, indeed, gratuitous.

What, then, in summary, is salvation for Baudelaire as the Christian tragic hero? Again, a relatively minor poem, not at all the equal of his great efforts, tells us explicitly the relationship of the two selves in this most complex *homo-duplex,* whose sadomasochism (while it exists) has so tragically misled so many exquisite critics, including Georges Blin himself. Baudelaire, as Arthur Symons and Algernon Charles Swinburne first pointed out, was above all "un poète de la débauche." We are very much afraid that the initial impression of Baudelaire as a "décadent farouche" in the lineage of Gautier's "l'art pour l'art" was generally more accurate than the current depiction of Baudelaire as "Saint Charles, le catholique dévoué." We refer to "L'Examen de minuit":

> *La pendule, sonnant minuit,*
> *Ironiquement nous engage*
> *A nous rappeler quel usage*
> *Nous fîmes du jour qui s'enfuit:*
> *—Aujourd'hui, date fatidique,*
> *Vendredi, treize, nous avons,*
> *Malgré tout ce que nous savons,*
> *Mené le train d'un hérétique.*

> *Nous avons blasphémé Jésus,*
> *Des Dieux le plus incontestable!*
> *Comme un parasite à la table*
> *De quelque monstrueux Crésus,*
> *Nous avons, pour plaire à la brute,*
> *Digne vassale des Démons,*
> *Insulté ce que nous aimons*
> *Et flatté ce qui nous rebute;*

> *Contristé, servile bourreau,*
> *Le faible qu'à tort on méprise;*
> *Salué l'énorme Bêtise,*
> *La Bêtise au front de taureau;*
> *Baisé la stupide Matière*
> *Avec grande dévotion,*
> *Et de la putréfaction*
> *Béni la blafarde lumière.*

> *Enfin, nous avons, pour noyer*
> *Le vertige dans le délire,*
> *Nous, prêtre orgueilleux de la Lyre,*
> *Dont la gloire est de déployer*
> *L'ivresse des choses funèbres,*
> *Bu sans soif et mangé sans faim! . . .*

*—Vite, soufflons la lampe, afin
De nous cacher dans les ténèbres!*

Midnight, in this admirable poem, is more than the bewitching hour for illicit lovers. It is the eternal moment of time in, as the Church Fathers once wrote, "this present evil aeon." And what existential option does Baudelaire, as our Christian tragic hero, truly and effectively make after his "examen"? He chooses carnal love, wine, drugs, debauchery, not God. Thus he damns himself forever as spiritual man. Baudelaire, despite his facile pretensions, was not really a mystic who, properly, in the true guise of authentic mysticism, sought to incorporate himself into the Infinite (or, rephrased, God), as all the great Catholic saints did. Instead, he is a cultist of the merely mysterious, who seeks to incorporate the cosmos into himself, into his romantic ego, into his decadent sensibility, just as all the great egotists and decadents did and yet do. Is it any wonder, then, that we must vote with Symons, Swinburne, and Oscar Wilde, closer in time and temperament to the real Baudelaire, who saw in him something of a Satanist and "décadent farouche," who sought to "épater le bon bourgeois" even more than Gustave Flaubert?

As Catholics ourselves, we take no joy in pointing out that Baudelaire was a bad and probably insincere Christian—bad because he was insincere, not merely faithless or immoral. It in no wise discomfits us, despite the preposterous religious claims for Baudelaire by otherwise competent and even perspicacious critics. He was no saint; he was carnal man. But we are professors who take infinite pleasure in the demonstrable fact that he sinned so exquisitely for our own aesthetic and perhaps truly spiritual edification in his *Fleurs du mal* and other works. Unlike T.S. Eliot, we do not place Baudelaire on the spiritual level of a Dante Alighieri.

Yet, unlike T. S. Eliot, whose literary orthodoxy kept him from what seemed to be an extravagant and even sacrilegious claim, Charles Baudelaire is the literary Dante of our postromantic period; for the architecture and pure artistry of *Les Fleurs du mal,* his one masterpiece, are devastatingly inimitable: original. He even seems to succeed more as a conscious and ever self-conscious artist as he loses his immortal soul to degradation, to despair, to gamier and gamier levels of debauchery in decadent *faisandage,* not as a Catholic saint (certainly) but rather as a Catholic existentialist *manqué,* paralyzed in his religious will as his syphilitic body was paralyzed in fact in a gloriously decadent (hence, properly aesthetic, for what is decadence but art, pure art) decline and fall that assumed metaphysical dimensions for all men.

Claudel as Christian Tragic Hero

We realize, of course, that Paul Claudel was a prolific writer = plays, essays, poems, Biblical exegeses, even a kind of apocalyptic literature. But it is Claudel as Christian tragic hero, revealing himself as a composite through his protagonists, both male and female, who interests us exclusively here. And since these protagonists are best seen in his major plays, we shall limit ourselves to their consideration, so that we may try to gain a new appreciation of the author, possibly not as a mystic, since mysticism is not really at the heart of Catholic Christianity, but rather as a hard-nosed Christian, trying daily to make his existential options for good and not for evil in the sacred quest of all Christians for the Kingdom, the Power, and the Glory.

In his plays, the central theme is love, whether carnal love, emotional love, or Christian love. For love, as *caritas,* is at the very heart of Christianity. Love, indeed, is divine justice, which has no other real *raison d'être.* In itself, love differentiates Christianity from Judaism, which, as Professor Arnold J. Toynbee and others have pointed out, is not so much a religion as a legalistic code of ethnocentric ethics. Certainly, justice, not love, is the abiding concern of Judaism and Jewry. In this light, too, in the full lineage of Hammurabi, another Semite, justice is mostly an eye for an eye and a tooth for a tooth. Christianity, with its more humane and humanistic Stoic roots, emphasizes love and forgetting and forgiving, however.

We think it would be a mistake to see in Claudel a "great Catholic mystic," though he was of course (to a certain extent) a Catholic visionary. One does not properly live his Christianity in the trances of religious exaltation, though all true Christian believers are occasionally capable of them. Instead, one lives his Christianity painfully on a diurnal basis, sometimes in existential despair and nausea, as he tries to opt for good and not for evil and thus extricate himself from the existential thinginess of life: the viscosity, as the existentialists say of the human condition. Claudel's plays, therefore, are profoundly existentialist in the Catholic tradition of Jacques Maritain and Simone Weil, a Jew who converted to Catholicism. He knew their works well and was both vocally and verbally sympathetic with the substance of their Catholic message.

Let us now begin our consideration of what we think to be Claudel's three greatest plays, *L'Annonce faite à Marie, Partage de midi,* and *Le Soulier de satin,* each of which intrigues us for a different reason. Certainly, together, they constitute the evolution of Paul Claudel's essential character, when his initial agnosticism gave way to a consuming Catholicism, ever concerned with *caritas* and with *koinonia.* By focusing our attention on these three remarkable dramas, then, we feel we can apprehend the incredible totality of Claudel's Catholic spirit. In the end, we hope our readers will understand why we claim that Claudel was not only one of the literary glories of France but also, even more significantly, as Claudel would have wished it, a sincere Christian, a noble man, whose sole *hamartia* (if such, indeed, his mole of nature may be called) was that he loved literature so ineffably much that it kept him from his religious vocation.

Consequently, he always felt guilty about his love for literature, and in truth he was a little embarrassed by it. For he would have loved nothing better than to be a simple *curé de campagne,* and in itself that was a mark of his Catholic grandeur in a Catholic mystique. Did he not always prefer to the intellectuals the simple people, who through their existential options daily practiced and lived their vibrant Catholic Christianity?

Though critical opinion states that *Le Soulier de satin* is Claudel's masterpiece, we tend to prefer far more the personal *Partage de midi,* since it represents a critical period of carnal love in Claudel's life as a committed Catholic. At the same time, we believe that *L'Annonce faite à Marie,* Claudel's first great play, was from a dramaturgical point of view his most successful. Moreover, we incline to think it will be absorbed into the canon of recognized French masterpieces, while *Partage de midi* will interest the biographer and student, and *Le Soulier de satin* will absorb only the erudite scholar, in the baroque manner of the Renaissance from which it derives its inspiration.

There were three versions of *L'Annonce faite à Marie,* of which the third and final version of is the one we shall consider. The scene takes place in the High Middle Ages, precisely at the apogee of Catholic Christianity, before it begins to suppurate in the fatal *faisandage* of doubt, deception, fragmentation, and compartmentalization. The Renaissance, with its deception and existential despair and concomitant nausea, is already in the air, as the stage is set for 1475 or so.

The principal protagonist is Pierre de Craon, a master architect, obsessed with building churches as eternal monuments to the eternal Catholic faith. A year before the scene opens, Pierre has tried to rape Violaine, who managed to escape with a knife wound on the arm. The following day, in an act of divine punishment, he contracted leprosy. He set off for Reims, there to build a church called Saint Justice, to thank god for the town's prosperity. However, France and all Christendom were suffering difficult times. There were two and sometimes three claimants to the papacy. Too, France was sundered by the English occupation and the incredible, ineffable weakness of Charles VII.

Engaged to Jacques Hury, Violaine is so consumed by the ardor of the Catholic faith that she contributes her *bague de fiançailles* to the Church. Pierre withers upon the vine both bodily and spiritually. Yet he loves her. In deep sympathy, she kisses him goodbye forever, unconsciously observed by her wicked sister, Mara, and thereby contracts the fatal leprosy that will ultimately destroy her but also simultaneously ennoble her. At length, Violaine confronts her fiancé, Jacques, with her leprosy, showing him the white splotch beneath her breast. At first, Jacques doubts her chastity, but since he loves her so desperately, he finally relents and forgives her in one of the most moving scenes of all world literature.

What does all this mean in terms of the existential option necessary in Catholic commitment for *engagement?* From the very outset, Claudel has cleverly foreshadowed the ineluctable dénouement of the starkest tragedy ever written outside Greek literature: tears, suffering, the gift of the engagement ring, the innumerable oblique references to the spiritual life that Violaine has already envisioned for herself in a kind of psychological *envergure.* What, however, does this mean in terms of the psychological drama? Emphatically, Claudel seems to state that in a spiritual sense Violaine could not yet accept her spiritual destiny, which God writes for every individual man and woman. In a spiritual sense, too, she must metamorphose herself—and, becoming a saint, truly embrace the metaphysical dimensions of her own suffering.

Violaine and Mara's father, Anne Vercors, also seeks spiritual release. He departs for a pilgrimage to Palestine, the Holy Land of Christianity. Thus, his vocation, like Violaine's, leads to an etherealized spiritual realm. Eight years pass. Then, on Christmas Eve, Mara seeks out her leprous sister with her dead child with her injunction as a Christian believer, committed for the moment, to resuscitate her dead daughter, Aubaine. In something of a trance, Violaine resuscitates the child at dawn and holds it to her leprous breast in her dirty shawl. Aubaine opens her eyes. Once they were black like Mara's, but now they are blue like Violaine's. Miraculously, too, Aubaine's lips are beaded with milk, as if from Violaine's leprous breast. At the same time, Charles VII and Joan of Arc have passed by in a cortège for his coronation at Reims Cathedral. In a fit of rage, Mara, as a terrible sinner, actually murders her saintly sister, as Claudel seems to say that "in this present evil aeon" (to use the very words of the original Church Fathers) the World, the Flesh, and the Devil, hélas, all too readily and far too often triumph over the Kingdom, the Power, and the Glory.

Mara, to be sure, finds eternal perdition. However, Anne, Pierre, and Violaine find salvation, even in the horrible state of negative justice that then applied in both the kingly and papal courts. Yet, enigmatically, perhaps even problematically, it is not earthly justice that prevails in Claudel's dramaturgical masterpiece. Rather, it is cosmic justice, though in earthly terms Anne, Pierre, and especially Violaine are Christian tragic heroes. Cosmic justice, in the end, always triumphs—as the Kingdom, the Power, and the Glory—over earthly justice, the World, the Flesh, and the Devil. Therefore, the Christian tragic hero is transfigured, just as in the tragic dénouement of *L'Annonce faite à Marie* Violaine becomes such a calendar saint that she can actually perform incredible miracles, even to the resuscitation of the dead. Now, Protestants do not all believe in miracles, but all Catholics do, emphatically, and Violaine is clearly a saint in the recognizable lineage of Catholic Christianity.

In our opinion, *Partage de midi* is Claudel's masterpiece, precisely because it is the most personal literary document he ever wrote—almost autobiographical, in fact—while at the same time it concerns universal dimensions for man and woman, caught up in the thinginess, or viscosity, of their existential despair and nausea. The plot is baldly simple. It is the story of Ysé, woman, or Woman, and Mesa, man, or Man, who chance across each other on a boat bound for the Orient. Mesa, a devout Catholic who has tragically just been refused a vocation, is a customs official. Ysé, a highly romantic type, quite etherealized yet also profoundly carnal, is the wife of an engineer name De Ciz. Ysé and De Ciz are accompanied by their children. Amalric, a soldier of fortune. DeCiz's good friend and Ysé's sometime lover, is also on board. He is strong while De Ciz is weak, and Ysé is psychologically repelled by her husband's weakness.

All four central characters are in their thirties, just before the sudden onslaught of middle age. Mesa is a bachelor, very glum, quite isolated in his spiritual malaise. The initial scene is on a hot day at high noon: hence the title, "Partage de midi." They have just passed Suez and entered on the sultry sea of the eternal Indian Ocean.

Mesa strides up to Ysé, who tips off her essential character as she reads a love story in her deckchair. Quite casually, yet with profound *sous entendus,* they talk about love in the abstract, while at the same time they have the concrete particularities and peculiarities of their own nascent liaison acutely on their minds. Later, in Hong Kong, Mesa momentarily turns his back on God and embraces Ysé in carnal love, just as Claudel had a fatal liaison with a bewitching Englishwomen. Why does Mesa contract this *liaison dangereuse?* Lust? We think not, really. Rather, it is his desire for revenge against a Semitic God for having denied him the vocation he thinks he wants most in this vale of tears, the World, the Flesh, and the Devil. So it is that guilt motivates him and causes his sin.

Like David with Bathsheba, getting rid of Urias the Hittite, Mesa sends De Ciz away on a dangerous mission, where he conveniently dies. Ysé hesitates and tries to talk him into remaining with her, but he goes anyway despite her repeated entreaties and importunities. She succumbs to Mesa: in fact, almost seduces him. She gets pregnant by Mesa, but then she decides to leave him for Amalric, a far stronger and far saner man.

Chinese revolution is at hand. Rather than let Ysé and her child fall into the hands of the rapist revolutionaries, Amalric dynamites the house. But Mesa miraculously appears, almost in a deus ex machina, with an exit permit. Amalric attacks him, tries to kill him, and then leaves with Ysé to board a ship for freedom. Yet, before the ship departs, Ysé murders her child by Mesa, since she wants a total break with the guilty past. Miraculously, Mesa revives, for he did not die.

This is the famous song of "Le Cantique de Mesa," which might very well have come from the "Song of Songs." It recaptures Claudel's tortured, involuted *état d'âme,* as he makes his existential option for God and spiritual love in his existential despair and nausea. Ysé, as a Christian, is also transfigured in the moment of truth of a Catholic existentialist. She makes her own existential option for God and for spiritual love, now incarnate in the sacrifice of her life that she is prepared to make for Mesa as an unworthy human receptacle of that divine love. She returns to Mesa. Of course, their love was wrong, even un-Christian. Yet is was psychologically right, and so it had its spiritual element, too, its undeniable spiritual value for two psychological beings.

They prepare to die in the dénouement, but we know they do not die in existential despair. For they have made the right existential options for love: for God incarnate in that love, even as the angelic part of a base, carnal liaison. They are transfigured: metamorphosed by their love for God. Indeed, they die, but as regenerated Catholics they die victoriously.

This play—in our opinion, Claudel's best—is highly poetic. It contains all the familiar Claudelian themes. Immediately, we recognize this is a kind of *Divine Comedy,* in which Claudel (like Dante) descends into the existential hell of human emotions and carnal weaknesses, while Ysé (or Beatrice) transfigures him through her essential goodness and mystically, through her love, leads him ultimately to Paradise, after he makes the right existential options. In the end, sadly, perhaps problematically, we have a kind of "partage de minuit," a parting at midnight, as the antipode to the "parting at noon" in the beginning. Night descends. We are left in human darkness, as Claudel seems to say. Yet, suddenly, we are inundated with the divine light of God, as Claudel (Mesa) glimpses God, like Dante in "Paradiso," just as Ysé (Beatrice) has brought him to God through a fatal carnal love that had its undeniable spiritual dimensions as a catalyst to and for divine love.

At once, for those of us familiar with Claudel's life (as recorded in Louis Chaigne's *Paul Claudel: The Man and the Mystic*), we recognize this autobiographical incident transmuted into immortal literature. Claudel did not die physically, but he did die in his old Adamic self. Henceforth, he is fire from flint: from God's flint, too. He burns like a true Catholic. Now most of us in Catholic Christianity, as well as many of our Protestant brethren, recognize how strong he became through his wavering faith in God, but we feel that Claudel has never been properly appreciated in his true dimensions as a Catholic existentialist. Hence, this is our position here and now: that he was, indeed, a Catholic existentialist, ever concerned with the critical importance of opting for the Kingdom, the Power, and the Glory, not for the World, the Flesh, and the Devil.

As a matter of fact, Mesa initially made the wrong option. But later he certainly opted for God—and the goodness of life in and through God's infinite mercy to man. Can anyone do more than make the right option for God's mercy, forgiveness, reconciliation? Did not Saint Augustine traverse the same road from carnality to God? Can we, then, not understand and forgive Claudel for the one seeming moment of weakness in what was surely a singularly blameless life?

It is ironic that the full body of critical opinion has fairly canonized *Le Soulier de satin* as "undeniably Claudel's finest work." We do not agree. In the dramaturgical sense, it was clearly *L'Annonce faite à Marie,* which will probably be restaged from age to age as long as there is a Comédie Française. At the same time, we also feel that *Partage de midi* is Claudel's admitted masterpiece because he so admirably combines the autobiographical element in a metaphysical message for all mankind. Moreover, we also feel that *Le Soulier de satin,* which has unjustifiably received such encomia, is not the essential Claudel—either medieval, or autobiographical, or markedly existentialist—but rather a baroque appendage to his Catholic work, glittering (to be sure) like the white tip of the iceberg, very much in the agnostic Renaissance tradition, while his truly more Catholic work remains submerged in *Cinq grandes odes,* the plays, and the Biblical exegeses. Still, though somewhat against the grain, we propose to analyze and synthesize this remarkable drama now.

Certainly, *Le Soulier de satin* is his summa, but that is just our point. It is too full to be effective, much less great, drama. In this light, for instance, let us discuss the overly elaborate plot, itself too much concerned with detailed action and too little concerned with the niceties of symbolic protrayal and the psychological depictions of Christian souls on fire.

If Claudel meant for the Renaissance to be the symbol of Christ's conquest of the earth, he surely erred. As all historians know, the Renaissance is more deeply rooted in Greco-Roman antiquity than in the kind of Catholicism epitomized by the High Middle Ages. The year is 1600 during the Spanish Conquest of the New World, but the play is extremely anachronistic.

The essential plot, stripped of all subplots, concerns Prouhèze, who is married to Pélage, a far older man—indeed, old enough to be her father. Her husband is aware of this and of the fact that Camille, a renegade, loves Prouhèze no less than Rodrigue. Thus, Pélage sneds her with Camille as his lieutenant to support the African fortress of Mogador. As a kind of Renaissance Rimbaud, Rodrigue proposes to Prouhèze that they run off together, but she rather curtly refuses. It is the Virgin Mary who has supported her against her carnal desire and emotional weakness. She opted for spiritual purity, her chastity, for the Madonna, and gave her satin slipper to the statue of the Virgin, from which symbolic act we derive the memorable title.

Essentially, the aesthetic problem is that *Le Soulier de satin* is far too much a spiritualized version of *Partage de midi.* As viceroy, Rodrigue sails for the New World and performs admirably for the King of Spain. Pélage, predictably, dies on a most convenient schedule. Prouhèze notifies Rodrigue of this death in a letter of commitment, which is lost for ten years. In the meantime, she marries Camille and bears a child, Sept-Epées. Eventually, however, Rodrigue comes to Mogador to keep his predestined Appointment in Samarra, just as the Arabs surround and menace Mogador. Prouhèze, consumed by Christian guilt for her carnal desire, rejects Rodrigue, though we are not sure we understand her real reasons any more than the hapless Rodrigue does.

Then, all to conveniently, in a kind of deus ex machina, Prouhèze dies, though she has entrusted Rodrigue with her beloved daughter, Sept-Epées. Then Rodrigue loses court favor and all his money. Like Rimbaud, he has lost a leg, his in combat, while Rimbaud lost his to cancer. Eventually, Sept-Epées married Juan d'Autriche. Finally, Rodrigue, in existential despair, though also in a Catholic *engagement,* becomes a porter in a convent. Only then, without a terrestrial love object, can he understand how Destiny, in the divine scheme of a living God, directed and ordered his incredible and truly tragic life. Always his great love was not for Prouhèze (or Beatrice) but rather for the Church, which Woman represented to him, and most of all for God (which Prouhèze also represented in her symbol and function as Love). At last, he finds spiritual contentment in a kind of Stoical or Buddhistic release from desire. He is metamorphosed. He is transfigured. Triumphantly, he finds God. To this extent, he ceases to be a Christian tragic hero, for he does not lose. He wins.

As we conceive of this dramatically unsatisfactory play, there is only one possible point of unity throughout the century it embraces—or, rather, pretends to embrace: the presence of God. As a Catholic, each protagonist relates to God in a different and even unique way, whether satisfactorily or unsatisfactorily. In all, there is a feeling of Christian oneness: of Catholic totality: of catholicity: yes, indeed, of true, historical, present, ever immanent Catholicity.

Professor Harold A. Waters concludes, in his *Paul Claudel,* that the play "redounds with optimism and hope." We cannot agree. Certainly, the Christian tragic hero is ennobled, transfigured, metamorphosed. But his cruel social context in a hostile cosmos of the World, the Flesh, and the Devil emphatically overwhelms him. One aspires for heaven, yes, and the true Christian obtains it with a Christian death in a state of grace; and so we agree with Professor Waters in this respect. But in sober truth he must suffer the terrestrial hell of the World, the Flesh, and the Devil in order to possess the Kingdom, the Power, and the Glory of God Eternal, acting existentially in the affairs of men in the sordid state known as the human condition.

What can we conclude of *Le Soulier de satin,* and by extension about Claudel, and, even more importantly for the specific purpose of this essay, about the Christian tragic hero? Certainly, this play is his emotional *adieu,* not only to the theater but also to his poetic imagination. In this sense, it is a summa of all that he has experienced in life and learned from it; as such, it is emphatically impressive. "Existence," in the existentialist sense, is ultimately resolved in the play when the Christian tragic hero, first opting for the illusion of carnal love, as once did Claudel, finally opts for *caritas* and *agape* in and through and of God Eternal, renouncing forever the temptations of the World, the Flesh, and the Devil. He, the Christian, attains the serenity of a saint. Claudel ceases to write imaginative literature now, first because he is an old man sickened by the flesh, but also because he wants to devote his waning years to Biblical exegeses.

We can understand that. We can accept it. But since we are Catholic critics primarily concerned with his imaginative literature, we also rue it.

What is our final assessment of Claudel? He was a good writer, sometimes a great writer, though infrequently; he was sometimes a good Chrisitian, always an impassioned Catholic, and, in the end, a great Catholic, even something of a saint. Truly, he embraces Catholicity and gives us the impression of having lived fully and intensely, while T. S. Eliot, an Anglo-Catholic (and we consider him only a different kind of Catholic), as our Christian counterpart, has only read widely and intently and not (we fear) lived at all except in the surrogate world of books, often dusty, never really satisfactory. Eliot is too cerebral for us in his Catholicism, but Claudel is never too indelicately carnal for us, and both men are great Catholics.

But while Eliot celebrates High Mass at Christmas at Canterbury Cathedral (and it is breathtakingly beautiful), the high point of the year for him is always at the martyrdom of Saint Thomas à Becket; and though an innovator who lifted liberally from the French symbolists, Eliot, as a Catholic, is, we fear, only looking at Dante's beautifully static Catholic past. As François Villon (another devout and carnal Catholic) would say, "où sont les neiges d'antan?" But Claudel is always High Mass on Easter Sunday at St. Peter's Basilica in the Vatican in Tomorrow's World, as Catholicism constantly changes and defines and redefines itself with its own existential options. For Claudel is truly a Catholic existentialist, and therefore kinetic, while Eliot is not—and therefore is static in a static universe. Eliot *is*; Clandel *becomes*. And what is the world for us Catholics if not, to paraphrase Goethe and Nietzsche—a Protestant and an atheist, both great Germans and imperfect internationalists—our Eternal Becoming in God's world, controlled for the moment by the Devil in the Flesh? As such, it is Claudel's paean to a ever-joyful Christian, Catholic world. And that is precisely *le mot juste*, in the Flaubertian sense, that best describes Claudel: joy.

King Arthur as Christian Tragic Hero

As in the case of Charlemagne, we apprehend the majestic figure of King Arthur only obliquely as he moves through the immortal literary saga of Camelot, which vanishes in the end almost as surely as if it had stepped from the libretto of *Finian's Rainbow*. Does this really surprise us? Indeed, it is a familiar and also formidable literary stratagem from a master storyteller's ample bag of literary tricks. One does not state; one only implies. Is this not truly a craftsman's best effort for poetic effect: not to state: but rather to imply: and to gain a relished impact through oblique allusion?

If we do not depart too much from our central idea in our impressionistic essay, let us quote three stanzas from "The Lady of Shalott" by Lord Tennyson, who may very well have been the greatest word magician in any language since Vergil in classical Latin. We cite these stanzas not to wax diffuse but rather to illustrate our central thesis about King Arthur: that, indeed, he was in Camelot the mirror that reflected the images of the other protagonists, Lady Guinevere, Lancelot, Tristan, Gawain, Galahad, Yvain, the enigmatic Merlin, and the mysterious Morgan le Fay. What, in a word, holds all these disparate figures together except that they are reflected (as passing images upon Camelot) upon the burnished mirror of King Arthur, as Lord Tennyson, writing also about Arthur in "The Idylls of the King," wrote in the singularly aesthetic "Lady of Shalott": almost in perfect reference to King Arthur, ever the symbol and unifying force in legendary Camelot:

> *There she weaves by night and day*
> *A magic web with colors gay.*
> *She has heard a whisper say,*
> *A curse is on her if she stay*
>   *To look down to Camelot.*

She knows not what the curse may be,
And so she weaveth steadily,
And little other care hath she,
 The Lady of Shalott.

And moving through a mirror clear
That hangs before her all the year,
Shadows of the world appear.
There she sees the highway near
 Winding down to Camelot;
There the river eddy whirls,
And there the surly village churls,
And the red cloaks of market girls,
 Pass onward from Shalott.

But in her web she still delights
To weave the mirror's magic sights,
For often through the silent nights
A funeral, with plumes and lights
 And music, went to Camelot;
Or when the moon was overhead,
Came two young lovers lately wed:
"I am half sick of shadows," said
 The Lady of Shalott.

Arthur is King of a Realm of Sunshine and Shadows, the very definition of life (in existential action) at Camelot. He is the sun at Camelot, just as surely as after him Louis XIV was the sun king at Versailles. In this sense, Arthur's protagonists in the saga are his shadows, and each shadow signifies a different aspect of Arthur as, like the god Apollo, he moves across the pristine blue British skies of Camelot. Let us take a look, then, in the Lady of Shalott's magical mirror, and analyze Guinevere and Lancelot and Tristan and Galahad and Merlin, and then synthesize how each adds a dimension of intuited poetic insight into our central figure, King Arthur, as the Christian tragic hero of legendary and ineffably beautiful Camelot, now lost to us among the willow wands of pure memory in time and space somewhere in South Albion.

But before we begin to recount our impressions, let us situate King Arthur in his legendary Camelot. Of course, we recognize that the authoritative study is still James Douglas Bruce's *The Evolution of Arthurian Romance from the Beginnings Down to the Year 1300.* We regret that this book is long on analysis, through abstruse textual emendations, and woefully short on synthesis and appreciation. Apparently, as if by definition, most scholars cannot see the forest for the trees, for Professor Bruce was a man who waxed eloquent and even verbose about King Arthur without ever once discussing the beauty (or even the meaning) of Camelot. For a specialized study, Professor Madeleine Pelner Cosman's *The Education of the Hero in Arthurian Romance* is not quite so aesthetically offensive; for while it justly pretends to scholarship, it yet perceives beauty behind mere words and meters. Regrettably, John Rhys, as in his *Studies in the Arthurian Legend,* is the sort of scholar who drove his students to frenzy, for he loses himself in a Welsh welter of qualifications, considerations, and conjectures in the proverbial forest among the proverbial trees. Jessie L. Weston's much overrated *From Ritual to Romance* still dazzles the undergraduate mind, just as it impressed the immature T. S. Eliot in his chaotic *Wasteland,* but it is really only bargain-basement Sir James George Frazer (*The Golden Bough*), with a limited application to our King Arthur in his fabled Camelot.

On a somewhat more auspicious note, Richard L. Brengle has given us *Arthur King of Britain: History, Romance, Chronicle, and Criticism,* a notable popularization of a difficult topic and a meandering period in English literature. Naturally, we do not praise it because it is a popularization but rather because it is clear, and clarity is what we emphatically need in the luxuriant undergrowth of esoteric Arthuriana, intelligible only sometimes to the medievalist and almost never to the interested and curious generalist.

Yet we are not prejudiced against "mere scholarship" because of its appreciative limitations in aesthetic practice and theory. Interestingly enough, we find that Professor Roger Sherman Loomis' *Arthurian Tradition and Chrétien de Troyes* is both scholarly and illuminative, as the best scholarship is always synthetically illuminative—and ever aesthetically appreciative, too. Mostly, however, in the European tradition, we prefer a considered *explication de texte.* For this reason, we have relied exclusively on Chrétien de Troyes' *Arthurian Romances* and Sir Thomas Malory's *Works,* as if they alone (and they are best) could be our guides through the veritable jungle of Arthuriana. We ever embrace simplicity: clarity. We ever eschew complexity: confusion. And was there ever anyplace where scholars could so completely lose themselves (and their good sense, if not professorial sanity) as in the miasmic swamp (surely another Okefenokee) of Arthuriana?

The first shadows in the magic mirror of Eternal Camelot come as King Arthur defines himself (in a preternatural consciousness and even self-consciousness of scarlet sin) in the adulterous love affair of his young wife, Queen Guinevere, with Sir Lancelot, a knight of the Round Table, while he, Arthur, is already an old man, tragically condemned to suffer such a terrible indignity in a tragic silence. We may blithely pass over Guinevere, who is not Arthur's foil (at least, when he was a young man like Lancelot), and turn to Sir Lancelot himself. He was the son of King Ban de Benoic. After his father's death, he was reared by Vivian, the enchanting Lady of the Lake. It was she who introduced him to King Arthur's court at imperial yet communist Camelot. There, he was made a knight of the Round Table. There, too, he distinguished himself by his heroic deeds. In time, he grew to love Queen Guinevere; then, unsatisfied with an etherealized chivalric love, he became her carnal lover in tragic fact. Thus, because of his horrible sin, the betrayal of King Arthur, even more than the venial sin of the flesh, he was adjudged unworthy to find the Holy Grail.

Instead, his son, Sir Galahad, found it. Galahad was the son of Elaine and the ablest and purest noblest knight of the Round Table (see the communism), thus alone adjudged worthy to locate the Holy Grail, the chalice from which Christ drank at the Last Supper in the Upper Room at Jerusalem. The many versions of Lancelot's end differ from one another. What really happened? Did he succeed to his father's throne after he slew King Claudas, only to be killed in turn by Modred, King Arthur's treacherous nephew? Or did he return, as we (romantics all) prefer to believe, to seek Guinevere after Arthur's death? And when he found that she had entered a nunnery in her existential despair, consumed by her existential nausea, did he (as we Christians prefer to believe) spend his remaining years at a hermitage to expiate for his adulterous betrayal of Arthur, not only his lord but also his friend and confidante?

Here, our triangle assumes a Christian dimension. We truly believe that Lancelot was consumed by guilt because he had betrayed his lord, his king, his friend, and that Guinevere felt guilty because she had betrayed a perfect husband too old to satisfy her desires. But what of King Arthur, our central concern in our impressionistic essay? What did he feel? How did her suffer? Did his suffering, in a word, make of him a better man, a better Christian? In response, we think it did: truly did. For we know from his reaction the keen and even cutting despair that he surely felt at learning that his beloved young wife, almost his daughter, had cut him to the spiritual quick by betraying him precisely with the man, Lancelot, whom he then loved most among the knights of the Round Table. But as the Greeks knew, "pain is gain," in the sense that wisdom, or courtly *sagesse,* comes from experience, or a confrontation with the evil of the World: the World, the Flesh, and the Devil in what the Church Fathers so rightly called "this present evil aeon," which admirably depicted even an ideal, or idealized, or idyllic Camelot, just as surely as it portrays Memphis, Tennessee, in the 1980s.

Yes, pain is gain. As Malory and Chrétien de Troyes relate the saga of Camelot, King Arthur suffered existential nausea, fell into the abulia of existential despair, because he was man: in a word, Man. But, he was more than man. He was a Christian, and in his existential Becoming, the Christian defines himself by the sum of his acts through his options. And what is Christianity, in summary, but love? After his betrayal, Arthur loved Guinevere and Lancelot not less, but in a different way, with an added dimension of *caritas* beyond more *eros,* and thus truly loved them more: as a Christian: in the sublime selflessness of Christian love: in its mercy, pity, compassion, and, above all, its existential commitment to forgiving and forgetting.

This, then, is the measure of Man when he is also a Christian. This is Christian magnitude: breadth: depth. This is Christian magnificence. This is existential *freedom:* when, as Arthur finally learns to do, he opts for selfless love: and, in losing self, transcends limitation through love and becomes a saint. For in the end King Arthur is also Saint Arthur. Is this not why we love him and remember him, too? The incredible strength of his Christian love (*caritas* in the *koinonia* of the Round Table and Camelot) transcended mortal self through an ennobling suffering: existentially to become Man: and, above all, existentially and also *essentially* to be a *Christian.*

Now we are ready for another love story to flit across the magic mirror of the Lady of Shalott in Camelot, surely our archetypal Urbs in "this present evil aeon." In our opinion, it is the most heartrending love story of all time, not only because Tristan did not get (possess forever) Isolde, whom he wanted, but also, and rather, because he did get (end up with) Isolde of the White Hands, whom he did not want. It was thus doubly tragic, was it not, among Merlin's shadows of the magic mirror of *Schein* and *Sein:* of appearance and reality, as the *Doppelgänger* would say and evidence. And if we have no romantic *Doppelgängers* in our saga of Camelot, we certainly see our quota of *homo-duplexes,* motivated by action and introspection, by *acte gratuit* and abulia.

Let us set the scene by baldly recounting the legend. Tristan is the son of Rivalin and King Mark's sister, Blanchefleur, foreshadowing and intimating both Isolde and Isolde of the White Hands. Both his parents die during his infancy. Consequently, Rual, a faithful liegeman, adoringly adopts Tristan and rears him like his own son. Afterward, Tristan is kidnapped for awhile, but he manages to escape. He goes to Cornwall to attend the court of a kindly

King Mark. Rual, at last, reveals his identity; but even before this happens, Mark's courtiers are impressed with him because of his ineffable charm: the charismatic personality, soon to reveal itself as the Great Lover. In quick succession, he recovers his father's lands and kills Moralt, an evil giant who has come over to exact tribute from Cornwall for Ireland. He even leaves a fragment of his sword in Morolt's sundered skull. Still, Tristan is tortured by a poisoned wound; he sets sail in a small boat for Ireland, where the queen, Morolt's mother, cures him in exchange for his tutoring her beautiful daughter, the fair Isolde.

Tristan, at length, returns to Cornwall, There, the barons, all jealous of his close relationship (even *camaraderie*) with King Mark, urge the king to marry. In response, Mark states he will marry only the lady whose golden strand of hair has been dropped rather conveniently and also symbolically be a swallow. That blonde lady, as it turns out, is none other than Isolde. Tristan wins her for Mark, even though the notch in his sword is discovered. En route back to Cornwall from Ireland, the pair drink a love potion intended for Mark's wedding night, and they simply cannot restrain their sexual passion for each other any longer.

On the wedding night, the maid Brangen substitutes for Isolde, but after several meetings with Tristan and their concomitant near discoveries, King Mark grows suspicious: jealous. He forces Isolde to take an oath (which she cannot possibly meet) and undergo the ordeal of hot iron. By a clever stragagem, she manages to escape. Still, Tristan is banished forever. Desperately, humanly, *menschlich all zu menschlich,* as Friedrich Nietzsche would say, he consoles himself with a coman surrogate (yet also *das ewige Weibliche*), Isolde of the White Hands, whom he marries. After several additional adventures, none germane to the legend, which vary greatly in the different versions, he is mortally wounded. His physicians, despairing of his life, summon Isolde in a desperate last effort to cure him by love while medical science has failed. But Isolde of the White Hands jealously exacts her fatal vengeance for being only second in Tristan's affections. Isolde comes in a ship with a white sail, signifying her love; but Isolde of the White Hands tells the dying Tristan that the ship has a black sail, meaning that she has refused to come and loves him no more. Thus, he dies, tragically enough, of a broken heart in a bittersweet moment of illusion and truth, of *Schein* and *Sein.* And the essence of the tragedy, in addition to the unrequited love of Isolde of the White Hands and the unfulfilled love of Tristan and Isolde, is the full measure of deception. For despite our psychiatric school of double-bind depth therapy, which argues that truth is unimportant, following Oscar Wilde on "The Necessity for Lying," is truth not the coequal of love and perhaps a dimension of the definition of love for the Christian? And here we are dealing with devout though carnal Christians in the chivalric mode of the Middle Ages.

From Shakespeare as well as from other Renaissance dramatists, we now call to mind the familiar device of dramatic foils in our effort to glimpse "sunlight" (poetic truth) in the Lady of Shalott's magic mirror in Camelot. In this sense, never explicitly, always implicitly, ever against the chameleon background of legendary Camelot, Arthur is Tristan's dramatic foil, i.e., a man who acts differently in the same circumstances. As a young man, Arthur knew carnal love no less than Tristan; and he opted for sex rather than spiritual love till he met Guinevere, his child wife, whom he loved more than life but not more than honor and far less than God, when he opted existentially for love in sex—and, in the end, love, despite the carnal connection. So, essentially, Arthur was once like Tristan to a certain specific and almost premeditated and certainly preternatural point: till that point in time when the foils diverged, as Hamlet contrasted with Laertes, and Tristan (disappointed in love) opted for death, while far more nobly Arthur (equally disappointed in love) opted for God, i.e., *caritas* in the *koinonia* of Camelot among his beloved and never macho and even effeminately chivalric knights of the Round Table.

In this sense, Tristan's life was tragic, for he chose carnal love and opted against Christian *caritas,* even with his faithful wife, Isolde of the White Hands. But also in this sense Arthur, though a Christian tragic hero, since he was defeated in love, and since the citadel of Camelot was destined to fall, was triumphant: beatifically triumphant. For was he not metamorphosed by existential despair (frustration and nausea over an adulterous wife) to find the hope of Christian salvation through his existential *engagement* to the selflessness of a totally desexed *caritas* in *koinonia*?

We end our impressionistic and quite heretical essay with Merlin, the famous prophet and magician, who, if there were a historical Merlin, probably lived in the fifth century. Let us recount baldly his life in the rather unpoetic terms he does not merit as a charismatic, enigmatic, and even problematic figure. He was born of a demon father, or incubus, i.e., a spirit who had sexual intercourse with women in their dreams, just as the succuba (the female principle, perhaps too *das ewige Weibliche*) had sexual relations with men in their dreams—and thus, at least in the Middle Ages, accounted for nocturnal emissions. His mother was a beautiful but doomed Welsh princess. It was Merlin, the boy without a father, who explained to King Vortigern why his tower would not stand, as he elaborated upon the ritual symbolism of the two serpents discovered under the foundation. He was a master of divination, and as a psychic he could predict the future. In fact, he did predict the future of Great Britan. Most importantly for our essay, he enabled through his magic Uther Pendragon to father Arthur, legendary King of the Briton, real and exact enough in fabled Camelot. Moreover, he was the spiritual adviser (at once Christian and profoundly pagan, or a Catholic with pagan roots) to the fifty knights of the Round Table, whom he personally helped Arthur select, not for the aggradizement of Camelot, but rather for the glorification of Catholic Christianity, since in a mystical sense the Arthur cycle is unified by its quest of the Holy Grail as much as by Arthur, who, really, incarnates that sacred quest fully as much as Sir Galahad. But what happened, in the end, to this omnipotent magician, who was the spiritual brains and psychological entrails behind Camelot? Alas, for the sake of his immortal soul, which he lost through a pagan obsession with magic, "mere magic," he was enslaved forever in a bush in the sacred wood of Brocéliande, the victim of a charm woven spiderlike (and black widow spiderlike, consuming her male) by Vivian, his mistress, ironically enough (or was it really ironic?) which he revealed to her in suicidal, existential despair at a beautiful world about to vanish, that of Camelot: precisely because he, Merlin, personified something of the incredible weakness inherent in the very strength, that of a carnal love (as for Vivian, as for Guinevere, as for Isolde) which tried ineffectually to coexist with *caritas* in the *koinonia* of the Round Table. So Merlin, too, failed: fails.

Indeed, in Camelot, a beautiful Utopia if there ever was one, they all fail: because they cannot actualize *caritas* in *koinonia,* consumed as they are by carnal love in a chivalric order that officially decries sexual passion: that is, all fail but two, Sir Galahad and King Arthur. Every good story needs a proper conclusion; and since Camelot is a terrestrial search for perfection, Galahad (as the noble man, totally desexed, and noble because he is desexed) must ultimately actualize perfection in the discovery of the Holy Grail. Yet, because he is so wretchedly anemic, Galahad is the least satisfactory protagonist of Camelot. Even Merlin knows carnal love, as do all the others in this fabulous sexual epic, subudued and attenuated though it is in its explicit eroticism. Even Arthur knows sexual love, or at least he has known the tragedy of carnal love and the triumph of *caritas* in *koinonia.*

But this is just our point: why Arthur, as we maintain, is our Lady of Shalott's magic mirror, who defines himself obliquely in terms of the shadows (the other protagonists) who flash upon it in the *pénombre* of Our Lady's tower. He has known carnal love—surprisingly, the one leitmotif of Camelot. But in his Christian dimensions he has surpassed it: gone quite beyond mere eroticism. In this sense, he is like Saint Augustine, who, too, knew carnal love and even debauchery before he opted for purity, as also with Galahad, who in his purity knew God: the Holy Grail. For Arthur was like Saint Augustine and not at all like Saint Thomas Aquinas, who seems never to have truly lived because in sober fact he appears never to have loved.

Arthur lived: intently: intensely. Arthur loved: intently: intensely. In truth, Arthur ultimately lived precisely and especially because he loved, had loved, and particularly loved Guinevere, who would love him as lord and father surrogate but not as man and husband. This, too, was a weakness: the great weakness, i.e., existential focus of affect on a love object that is person and not God. He was disappointed: in existential despair. He suffered nausea from the existential thinginess, or viscosity, of his Round Table in Camelot, which, though he loved it and lived for it, must surely have disgusted him in the end: revolted him. For in the end it was not Guinevere or the Round Table or Camelot that counted. Rather, it was God, symbolized by the Holy Grail—as if his Catholic commitment (his intellectual assent) to try to believe to believe; and, as with Saint Augustine, he found salvation through belief and in the state of grace engendered in the germinal act of that belief.

Arthur found belief, and he believed. He opted for God, not Guinevere or carnal love or Camelot (the World, the Flesh, and the Devil), and he found God. Despair became hope, and gratuitous action became meaningful *engagement.* Arthur, a human failure, a risible and tragic cuckold, died a saint. And that was the measure of him as a man, as Christian tragic hero. And that, though we are the first to verbalize it in the Occident, is why all us Christians yet love Arthur, in the problematic code of chivalry, at once etherealized and highly carnal, and why we will always study him: even more, relish him as the Saint Augustine he really is for us in our grand but rarely grandiose Christian tradition.

Chaucer as Christian Tragic Hero

At the outset, let us circumscribe a subject that, to be complete, would require not merely a volume but rather an encyclopedia. For the sake of compression, we deal exclusively with aspects of the Christian tragic hero in *The Canterbury Tales,* admittedly Chaucer's masterpiece but by no means his only significant work. Moreover, we do not assume that Chaucer is entirely the characters he depicts, for his humanistic *envergure* is far too great for that localization.

Still, facets of Chaucer's charismatic personality emerge in *The Canterbury Tales,* the first great realist work in English literature. In the end, we shall try to draw a composite picture of Chaucer as a Christian tragic hero in the waning days of the much misunderstood Middle Ages. Our protrait, of course, will be too highly impressionistic to please the strict textual scholars, but perhaps it will inspire them to refute our thesis, and in itself this will surely enrich the entrancing and unique world of Chauceriana.

To situate Chaucer in his cataclysmic age, we refer our readers to G. G. Coulton's erudite *Chaucer and His England,* a scholarly study, and also to Marchette Chute's most readable *Geoffrey Chaucer of England,* a popularization that is sometimes inexact but always entrancing. To crystallize Chaucerian criticism, we refer our readers to Edward Wagenknecht's *Chaucer: Modern Essays in Criticism.* Since *The Canterbury Tales* is Chaucer's avowed masterpiece, we signal out William Witherle Lawrence's *Chaucer and the Canterbury Tales* in this respect. Yet, to our mind, the most brilliant recent work is D. W. Robertson, Jr.'s *A Preface to Chaucer: Studies in Medieval Perspectives,* though the title is somewhat misleading, since Chaucer surely foreshadows the Renaissance far more than he epitomizes the Middle Ages. P. M. Kean's *Chaucer and the Making of English Poetry,* in two magnificent volumes, is simply incomparable. Our quotations are from F. N. Robinson's *The Works of Geoffrey Chaucer.*

We will not patronize our readers. We assume that many of them know far more about Chaucer than we do. But as Catholic critics, having embarked on religious studies of seminal writers, perhaps we can bring a Baudelairean *nouveau frisson,* if not new knowledge, to a constantly changing modern appreciation of Chaucer, our first great English writer.

First, let us situate Chaucer religiously in his own time, so that we may glimpse a better perspective of the Christian tragic hero. His dates are approximately 1340–1400, but he clearly foreshadows the Renaissance in several important respects, particularly realism and psychological amplitude. Certainly, Chaucer is no Dante, himself an epitome of the literary and religious values of the High Middle Ages. Emphatically, something happens in the spiritual crisis, or *Erwachung,* which was that fateful century between 1300 and 1400; and that something is incarnate in a psychological and religious sense in (surprisingly enough) our Christian tragic hero of Geoffrey Chaucer. How, in a word, is this radical reorientation, or transition, from the High Middle Ages reflected in *The Canterbury Tales?*

To be sure, the stories of *The Canterbury Tales* bear the familiar and recognizable imprint of Everyman in a religious quest that we hope leads to man's salvation at the feet of a merciful God. The scheme has been well codified. As stated in the Prologue, each pilgrim will tell four tales, two on the journey toward the sacred site of Canterbury and two on the way back. In this sense, it is a religious pilgrimage to England's most holy place, site of the assassination of the saintly Thomas à Becket, a great Catholic martyr to political machinations. But Chaucer did not finish the manuscript. Only twenty-three of the thirty pilgrims get a chance to tell their story. Moreover, some tales are left incomplete, and others are painfully maladapted to the tellers. If we may venture an aesthetic opinion, it is apparent that the stories of *The Decameron* entrance us, while the storytellers do not, whereas in *The Canterbury Tales* the storytellers ever interest us, while the stories are frequently boring. *The Canterbury Tales* is not, to our minds, the masterpiece that English literary history has tried to make of it for perhaps chauvinistic reasons based on inexact standards of literary evaluation. We doubt very much that it is the equal of Homer or the Poetic Edda or Vergil or Dante. Yet is is a great humanistic document of eternal human interest, and this is how we shall consider it in the dimensions of the Christian tragic hero.

For the Everyman motif in *The Canterbury Tales* is very Christian, very Catholic; these elements are demonstrably present, as in the Knight's Tale. At the same time, *The Canterbury Tales* is memorable as the first breath of fresh air from eternal spring that inundated the moribund and sometimes unhealthy Middle Ages from the blooming Renaissance, which appears circa 1445 with Gutenberg's movable print and with the cataclysmic fall of Constantinople in 1453. To our mind, in an analogy, what differentiates Renaissance literature from medieval literature, even in the latter's fullest expression of the *Roman de la rose* and, indeed, Dante's *Divina Commedia,* is that medieval literature is only two-dimensional. On the other hand, Renaissance literature, like *The Canterbury Tales,* that first fresh breath of pristine air, is richly multidimensional. "Rich," yes: Certainly, that word, more than any other, depicts the texture, if not the magnitude, or *envergure,* of *The Canterbury Tales.*

Perhaps the ineffable beauty of *The Canterbury Tales* can best be understood in terms of antipodes: the "World, the Flesh, and the Devil" of diurnal reality (*Sein*) and "the Power, the Kingdom, and the Glory" (*Schein*). In this respect, we know that the Miller's Tale and the vilest fabliaux represent "the World, the Flesh, and the Devil" in a manner of high comedy (yet, enigmatically, perhaps problematically too, low comedy), in the manner of the Middle Ages and the nascent Renaissance (*sic,* circa 1400) at the same time. Yet the Knight's Tale, as one of many notable stories, clearly shows the high manner of "the Power, the Kingdom, and the Glory," which has roots in the Middle Ages and (though somewhat transfigured) continues in the religious literature of the Renaissance itself. Clearly, allegory did not die one mythical day of literary metamorphosis; it merely grew and changed and developed. How it changed in terms of the Christian tragic hero may be discussed as: (1) fortune and free will; (2) marriage; and (3) the nobleness of man. Of course, the sophisticated reader recognizes these three categories from Professor Kean's admirable exegesis of Chaucer. But we shall discuss these categories in the specific terms of the Christian tragic hero, the composite of which (in the end) is Chaucer himself, the literary total who is far more than merely the sum of the parts, i.e., the individual portraits contained in the several tales.

For the Catholic Christian, perhaps the cardinal question in his religion is whether man has free will, and if he does, how it works. The Knight's Tale states this problem, examines it, offers a kind of philosophical solution. Yet this solution is perhaps more courtly and certainly more chivalric than specifically Christian and Catholic. The Man of Law's Tale uses the hagiographic romance to develop the expressed Christian solution to the moral dilemma of man and free will. Constance, as the Christian tragic hero, is emphatically the hapless victim of fickle Fortune and also of negative planetary positions. Yet, at the same time, she guards faithfully her freedom of will and ever exercises her existential options for Christian virtue. As a corollary, certainly against the deism to sweep Europe in the eighteenth century, God intervenes in nature against the malignant designs of fortune. Thus, the tale is profoundly Christian in its depiction of the tragic hero, triumphant spiritually as a saint over the adversities of the World, the Flesh, and the Devil. Yet, problematically, Chaucer, while opting for Catholic free will, seems to foreshadow Calvinistic predestination:

> *Peraventure in thilke large book*
> *Which that man clepe the hevene ywriten was*
> *With sterres, whan that he his birthe took.*
> *(The Man of Law's Tale, 11.190-96)*

While the tale is essentially Christian, it is also something of a Stoic document. In itself, this should not be surprising, for the noblest and most idealistic currents of Christianity come from Stoicism. Hence, Chaucer emphasizes that we should not be enslaved to our passions, while at the same time we must be involved (or make our existential options, as Heracleitus would say) in the inevitable chances and changes of a singularly transitory and kinetic world. These ideas are profoundly Stoic, as all readers of Zeno, Epictetus, and Marcus Aurelius will readily recognize. But Chaucer makes an effective observation, which we feel is profoundly Christian: that Stoic joy is rooted in "the joye of this world," which the Christian (tragic hero) finds "the joye that lasteth evermo."

In the Man of Law's Tale, it is Griselda, the patient Griselda, who is our Christian tragic hero, incomparably great (and Christian) because she has patience, or, as the Stoics thought of it, self-sufficiency, though in the Christian world view it is her mystical faith that is the motor force of her "Christian patience." In the end, Walter, the bovine ass of a husband, is reconciled to his exemplary wife, the patient and faithful Griselda. Indeed, Griselda is an earthly prototype of the Virgin Mary at the height of medieval reverence of the Virgin, which certain Protestants have misconstrued as mariolatry. Griselda, ultimately, loves (*caritas*) her husband into moral submission, tantamount to his recognition of her as his beloved wife. From our own standpoint, this tale of the patient Griselda is more allegorical and, thus, less humanistic than the coarsest of the fabliaux. Thus, while it interests us as a moving portrait of the Christian tragic hero, it is, indeed, less relevant to our sophisticated age, one of overripeness and even of *faisandage*.

The theme, in a word, is Fortune—and its relation to Christian free will, which Catholics have always prided themselves on. How does this relate to Stoicism? Certainly, the Stoic, as ideal classical man, had an inner self-sufficiency that stood him well against the vagaries and vicissitudes of fickle

Fortune. But that is just the point of difference between Stoic and Christian. The Stoic, while he believes in the *logos spermaticos* as well as in the mystical brotherhood of man, has, indeed, an inner strength apart from the outer reality of God, whereas the Christian receives his strength only in the form of faith in his existential option for God against the sinful "thinginess" of the World, the Flesh, and the Devil.

In the Nun's Priest's Tale, the central themes of fortune and free will are woven in this yet amusing burlesque of the cock and the fox. Chantecleer, the cock, is, as he thinks, ideally and idyllically situated with his harem of hens in a farmyard. What could possibly go wrong to wreak unhappiness upon our hero, who in a sense is something of a Christian tragic hero, a kind of Everyman blithely unaware of the presence of ill fortune? Chantecleer is especially content with his carnal lot with Pertelote, his favorite paramour among his hen harem. Yet, in the Garden of Eden, lies the apple; and man's innocence is soon to pass, as Chaucer succinctly says:

> *For evere the latter end of joye is wo.*
> *God woot that worldly joye is soon ago.*
> *(The Nun's Priest's Tale, 1. 3205-6)*

Nowhere is the problem of "necessity" (fate, or destiny) and free will more explicitly stated than in the following lines, rich in texture and scope and meaning:

> *Thou were ful wel ywarned by thy dremes*
> *That thilke day was perilous to thee;*
> *But what that God forwoot moot nedes bee,*
> *After the opinioun of certein clerkis.*
> *Witnesse on hym that any parfit clerk is,*
> *That in scole is greet altercacioun*
> *In this mateere, and greet disputisoun,*
> *And hath been of an hundred thousand men.*
> *But I ne kan nat bulte it to the bren*
> *As kan the hooly doctour Augustyn,*
> *Or Boece, or the Bisshop Bradwardyn,*
> *Wheither that Goddes worthy forwityng*
> *Streyneth me nedely for to doon a thyng, —*
> *"Nedely" clepe I symple necessitee;*
> *Or elles, if free choys be graunted me*
> *To do that same thyng, or do it noght,*

> *Though God forwoot it er that was wroght;*
> *Or if his wityng streyneth never a deel*
> *But by necessitee condicioneel.*
>   *(The Nun's Priest's Tale, 1. 3230-49)*

Destiny happens. Chantecleer, as the Christian tragic hero, is over-whelmed by a contretemps: bad luck: ill fortune. Perhaps Chantecleer, like Man, has a *hamartia,* i.e., his carnal lust, his devotion to the Flesh for the World and the Devil, much against the Kingdom and the Power and the Glory of God. Chantecleer, by analogy, was Adam in Paradise, or Every-man of the Middle Ages, or our hero of the nascent Renaissance. The animal of the burlesque is Man, or the Christian tragic hero, who must relate himself to Destiny (in Greek, *Wyrd*) and accept the guilt for making his wrong existential option (in Christian free will) before he can make atonement with God and find his salvation.

One of the seven sacraments of the Catholic Church is matrimony. So it comes as no surprise to us that Chaucer is interested in marriage and treats it in a number of tales that Professor George Lyman Kittredge was the first to call "the marriage group." Essentially, the problem lies in the nature of the partnership in marriage—or what Jean Giraudoux of our own twentieth century terms meaningfully "le Couple." In the Clerk's Tale and the Merchant's Tale, the man dominates the woman in "le Couple," while in the Wife of Bath's Prologue and Tale it is emphatically the woman who dom-inates. Now, the Knight's Tale, the Clerk's Tale, and the Man of Law's Tale are not sophisticated or courtly in their treatment of love. Nor is the Wife of Bath's Prologue, though her tale certainly has courtly leanings in it. Moreover, in different ways, with other voices and relevant points of view, both the Franklin's Tale and the Merchant's Tale use similar ideas as a point of philosophical and even religious reference in time and space.

The Franklin's Tale concludes Professor Kittredge's "marriage debate" in *The Canterbury Tales,* though in its relevance to the Christian tragic hero we want to consider it first. At once, Chaucer explicitly states the roles of man and woman in the Christian marriage:

> *. . . She fil of his accord*
> *To take hym for hir housbonde and hir lord,*
> *Of swich lordshipe as men han over his wyves.*
>   *(The Franklin's Tale, 1. 741-3)*

Ideally, the Christian marriage does not mean the end of love because, as he further states, each partner should be submissive to the other—or, better, mutually submissive *with* each other to the dominant ideal of Christian love. It is the love vision, the love ideal, that counts in Christian love, even in the dimensions of its carnal passion.

At the same time, there is a Catholic level of *amicitia* (companionship) along with *amor* (love). Yet, admittedly, such Christian love is only an ideal, perhaps an impossible ideal, too. Just as the Christian tragic hero will always sin, so, too, he will never realize such an ideal and impossible love; and to the extent that he cannot, he is a tragic hero in the very measure of his keen disappointment in his cutting existential despair. Too, as a result, he feels what the existentialists will later call "nausea."

In the Wife of Bath's Prologue and Tale, we enter a new world. Clearly, the adorably whorish Wife of Bath calls for woman's dominance in "le Couple." Bluntly, she describes the kind of husband she most desires in marriage:

> *Myn housbonde shal it have bothe eve and morwe,*
> *Whan that hym list come forth and paye his dette.*
> *An housbonde I wol have, I wol nat lette,*
> *Which shal be bothe my dettour and my thral,*
> *And have his tribulacion withal*
> *Upon his flessh, whil that I am his wyf.*
> *I have the power durynge al my lyf*
> *Upon his propre body, and noght he.*
> *Right thus the Apostel tolde it unto me;*
> *And bad oure housbondes for to love us weel.*
> *Al this sentence me liketh every deel"—*
> *(The Wife of Bath's Prologue, 1. 154-62)*

Of course, not interested in companionship, she does not wax eloquent over *amicitia*. But she emphatically does develop the idea of *amor* as "a great desire to know carnal pleasure with someone," preferably within the religiously allowed limits of Christian marriage, since she is in a profound sense a "carnal Christian," though her essential Christianity and the goodness of her whorish heart have not been sufficiently appreciated.

In her way, again as a good-natured whore, she loved, and gave to, all her five husbands; but she loved most the fourth and fifth for obvious reasons. Of the fourth she even says:

> *My fourthe housbonde was a revelour;*
> *That is to seyn, he hadde a paramour;*
> *And I was yong and ful of ragerye,*

> *Stibourn and strong, and joly as a pye.*
> *How koude I daunce to an harpe smale,*
> *And synge, ywis, as any nyghtyngale,*
> *Whan I had dronke a draughte of sweete wyn!*
> *Metellius, the foule cherl, the swyn,*
> *That with a staf birafte his wyf hir lyf,*
> *For she drank wyn, thogh I hadde been his wyf,*
> *He sholde nat han daunted me from drynke!*
> *And after wyn on Venus moste I thynke,*
> *For al so siker as cold engendreth hayl,*
> *A likerous mouth moste han a likerous tayl.*
> *In wommen vinolent is no defence, —*
> *This knowen lecchours by experience.*
>
> (The Wife of Bath's Prologue, 1. 453-68)

But the fifth was the great consuming love of her life, and she says of him with moisture in her mouth, salivating in her carnal desire:

> *Now of my fifthe housbonde wol I telle.*
> *God lete his soule nevere come in helle!*
> *And yet was he to me the mooste shrewe;*
> *That feele I on my ribbes al by rewe,*
> *And evere shal unto myn endyng day.*
> *But in oure bed he was so fressh and gay,*
> *And therewithal so wel koude he me glose,*
> *Whan that he wolde han my* bele chose,
> *That thogh he hadde me bete on every bon,*
> *He koude wynne agayn my love anon.*
> *I trowe I loved hym best, for that he*
> *Was of his love daungerous to me.*
>
> (The Wife of Bath's Prologue, 1. 503-14)

But is not carnality a proper dimension, too, of Christian love, at least for Catholics, though perhaps not for Puritans? The Wife of Bath, at least, was married; and so she was within her rights to demand carnal love as the proper marital expression of Christian joy. Still, mere carnality is not ideality. To the extent that the Wife of Bath is incapable of the purer dimensions of marriage in Christian ideality, she is (as Chaucer implies) something of a tragic hero: tragic, yes, because she cannot actualize herself in the mystical union of Christian marriage like most men, like most women, but rather loses herself in mere carnality.

The Merchant's Tale is also essentially concerned with the man-woman relationship, fundamental in Christianity. It is the story of January and May, a very particular and even peculiar couple, though their situation assumes universal dimensions and thus attains the poetic level of metaphysical truth. At first, January wants to get married only to focus his lechery on the love object in his wife. As an old man, he has suddenly metamorphosed into a sybarite, as Chaucer describes him in the following lines:

> *Whilom ther was dwellynge in Lumbardye*
> *A worthy knyght, that born was of Pavye,*
> *In which he lyved in greet prosperitee,*
> *And sixty yeer a wyflees man was hee,*
> *And folwed ay his bodily delyt*
> *On wommen, there as was his appetyt,*
> *As doon thise fooles that been seculeer.*
> *And whan that he was passed sixty yeer,*
> *Were it for hoolynesse or for dotage,*
> *I kan nat seye, but swich a greet corage*
> *Hadde this knyght to been a wedded man*
> *That day and nyght he dooth al that he kan*
> *T'espien where he might wedded be,*
> *Preyinge oure Lord to graunten him that he*
> *Mighte ones knowe of thilke blisful lyf*
> *That is bitwixte an housbonde and his wyfe,*
> *And for to lyve under that hooly boond*
> *With which that first God man and woman bond.*
>   (The Merchant's Tale, 1. 1245-62)

In continuation, let us consider now the most famous love scene in Chaucer, as it depicts January with May:

> *He was al coltissh, ful of ragerye,*
> *And ful of jargon as a flekked pye.*
> *The slakke skyn about his nekke shaketh,*
> *Whil that he sang, so chaunteth he and craketh.*
> *But God woot what that May thought in hir herte,*
> *Whan she hym saugh up sittynge in his sherte,*
> *In his nyght-cappe, and with his nekke lene;*
> *She preyseth nat his pleyyng worth a bene.*
>   (The Merchant's Tale, 1. 1847-53)

May is the counterpart of a modern call girl, all the more outrageous because she is legally a Christian wife and not a concubine, even within the medieval ethos. Once bought (and she is bought), she, like a good whore, gives sensual value for the money paid. At first, the situation is acceptable, though risible. But when January goes blind, he becomes even more possessive and jealous of May. Still, at this point, we, as readers, feel our first genuine sympathy for January, or Man, or Christian hero, since Man has a carnal nature, as does the Christian, and sometimes does foolish things to satisfy his lust, as does January. After all, didn't May marry for "coveitise," or money, making herself a whore, as perhaps all women have a price, though the price is not always money and may be idealism and may be marriage as the good life?

Finally, January sees May as she really is, consumed by greed, and has his moment of truth. But he desires her so much that abulia paralyzes his will. He is subjugated. Woman wins, as she frequently does, even usually does, in the man-woman relationship; and this is a dimension of the Christian tragic hero, too: that, though he is supposed to be the master in "le Couple," he is frequently a slave in a sadomasochistic double-bind that strips the marriage of its religious meaning of the mystical union of Christ (Man) with the Church (Woman).

Now, we are ready to consider the third and most important dimension of the Christian tragic hero in *The Canterbury Tales:* the nobleness of man, itself originally a Stoic doctrine, since we must never overlook the richness of Stoic contributions to early Christianity in the impact of the Greco-Roman world upon our Catholic faith.

The Canterbury Tales is ever great inasmuch as its focus is Man, and as it is a Catholic document, that means the Christian tragic hero. Too, Man, at his best, is noble; and just as Chaucer is sometimes preoccupied with man at his worst in the gross fabliaux, he also considers Noble Man, since Man as totality is only a little lower than the angels in the great chain of being.

Perhaps the Knight's Tale, since the Knight is a Noble Man, is his most noteworthy presentation of the Noble Man, or Theseus, or Christian tragic hero. He shows pity. He shows virtue, not even *ira,* or righteous anger. He is kingly, truly regal. He is "gentle," though not in the modern sense of that word. He is rational. He is prudent. He is magnanimous, as the most important facet of fortitude. For *vertu* is manhood and not at all modern "virtue," which is really negative since it means the absence of evil or undesirable qualities and means nothing positive in the possession of good qualities.

Many of the same qualities are found in the Physician's Tale, where the protagonist is a woman named Virginia. In the following speech, Chaucer describes the worth of physical creation as specifically existing for the proper worhsip of God in his celestial paradise:

> *Pigmalion noght, though he ay forge and bete,*
> *Or grave, or peynte; for I dar wel seyn,*
> *Apelles, Zanzis, sholde werche in veyn*
> *Outher to grave, or peynte, or forge, or bete,*
> *If they presumed me to countrefete.*
> *For He that is the formere principal*
> *Hath maked me his vicaire general,*
> *To forme and peynten erthely creaturis*
> *Right as me list, and ech thyng in my cure is*
> *Under the moone, that may wane and waxe;*
> *And for my werk right no thyng wol I axe;*
> *My lord and I been ful of oon accord.*
> *I made hire to the worshipe of my lord;*
> *So do I alle myne othere creatures,*
> *What colour that they han, or what figures.*
>
> (The Physician's Tale, 1. 14-28)

Virginia possesses the ideal qualities of Woman: chastity, humility, abstinence, temperance, patience, measure, discretion, wisdom, modesty, constancy, perseverance, sobriety, and innocence. In short, Virginia is the very embobodiment of Noble Man, both physically in her natural aspect and morally in her comprehensive endowment. Yet the tragedy, as so often happens in an absurb world, meaningless without relevance to God's Eternal Design, is that Virginia dies when she is only twelve. As a Christian tragic hero, she simply cannot survive her encounter with lechery. In itself, this seems to imply that a tragic dimension of the Christian hero is his inability to relate to the World, the Flesh, and the Devil, as separate from the Kingdom, the Power, and the Glory. Is this, indeed the *volte face* of the *moralitas* in the Physician's Tale? If it is, as we suspect, Chaucer is himself already in the Renaissance, rejecting the other worldliness of the High Middle Ages in which he participates, the waning of a great age.

Then what can we impressionistically surmise about Chaucer himself as a Christian tragic hero? We do not feel he was a good Christian in the medieval tradition, for he was already looking forward to the sensual luxuriance of the Renaissance. Still, we feel he had made his existential option to try to believe to believe, and that is all the Catholic Church has ever asked of her sons and daughters. He is alive. He is human, very human, perhaps all too human—

or, as the great anti-Christian Friedrich Nietzsche said, *menschlich all zu menschlich.* Ultimately, it is through his humanity that he will live forever in the hearts of English-speaking people. Yet an important part of that humanity is his Christianity, its Christianity: its presentation of the Christian tragic hero, caught in the hostile cosmos of the World, the Flesh, and the Devil, and fighting ever for the Kingdom, the Power, and the Glory.

We do not believe that Chaucer, however, can maintain his status as a giant of English literature, second perhaps only to Shakespeare in his poetic gifts and psychological understanding of man and woman. His poetry, indeed, is exquisitely beautiful, but it is in a Middle English no longer accessible to most modern readers, and the translations fail to indicate its lingering piquant beauty. Moreover, *The Canterbury Tales,* glorious as it is, yet is only an incomplete fragment, whose very incompletion causes us some concern. But the High Middle Ages is history, and in the modern world few of us can relate to a Thomistic Everyman on a spiritual quest, and even the Renaissance has receded into the dim purple shadow of a background. At one time, who would have thought that Edmund Spenser's *Faerie Queene* would one day be highly regarded only by overly cerebral scholars in dust-filled rooms of the recondite and receding past? Likewise, we feel Chaucer has reached the high watermark of his popularity in our own day.

We believe that, in a final surge of interest, we should study Chaucer as he has never really been studied before, his own Christian tragic hero when the Middle Ages met the nascent Renaissance on a country road to Canterbury. And then, sadly, Chaucer will not be very relevant to our constantly changing world, and we fear we will remember him mostly as the antipode to *Roman de la rose,* also fallen into popular oblivion and read only by the student and the scholar. For Chaucer's literary destiny, if we read the critical constellations aright, is to be one of the lesser luminaries of our literary firmament.

Impossible, you say?

Did it not happen to Spenser?

It is now to happen to Chaucer, too. But his requiem mass will be our study of his Christian dimensions, and we shall always remember him in this light as his own Christian tragic hero, an aspect of himself which as Renaissance courtier he could never accept, and at which, tragically, he probably smiled with the curling lips of a cold contempt.

Shakespeare as Christian Tragic Hero

Probably, more nonsense has been uttered about William Shakespeare than any other man who ever lived except Hitler, Stalin, Napoléon, and Alexander the God. He has been institutionalized in the English language as Homer was in Greek, Vergil in Datin, Dante in Italian, Molière in French, and Goethe in German, and perhaps Dostoevsky in Russian, Yet, according to our own objective correlatives, Shakespeare may be the most overrated writer of all time—not that he did not write brilliantly when he was at his best, but that he wrote so unevenly when he was not (as often) at his best.

Without recourse to an absurd image, let us baldly state the truth: Shakespeare wrote four great tragedies, three or four excellent histories, and a couple of good comedies, but the rest of his canon is glaringly unequal and often poor. In other words, nothing in all literature can surpass *Othello,* but *Coriolanus* is mediocre, and *Timon of Athens* is wretched, just as Shakespeare was mediocre most of the time and really execrable some of the time, perhaps to our own aesthetic astonishment.

The sheer volume of Shakespeareana is admittedly enormous. We shall cite only a few volumes of particular current interest, since most Shakespeareana is too erudite to interest the general reader and since some of it really reads like science fiction or outer-space fantasy. For an admirable glimpse into the Elizabethan *Zeitgeist*, we especially recommend Professor Karl J. Holzknecht's *The Backgrounds of Shakespeare's Plays.* For the biography, we feel no one has surpassed Professor Edgar I. Fripp's *Shakespeare: Man and Artist,* an ideal two-volume compendium. For a detailed study of the dramaturgy (and Shakespeare was a supremely skilled technician as well as a master psychologist), we recommend Professor Una Ellis-Fermor's *Shakespeare the Dramatist and Other Papers.* The best general biography seems to be A.L. Rowse's *William Shakespeare.* Of particular interest to us was Professor Lily B. Campbell's *Shakespeare's Tragic Heroes: Slaves of Passion.* For quotations, we have relied upon Professor Hardin Craig's *Shakespeare.*

Now, let us narrow our topic from Shakespeare's work as a whole to a consideration of the four great tragedies—*Hamlet, Macbeth, King Lear,* and *Othello*—specifically from the standpoint of the Christian tragic hero, which is somewhat different from what Professor Campbell did in her *Shakespeare's Tragic Heroes.* Although we believe Chaucer mirrors the Christian tragic hero in his *Canterbury Tales,* we doubt whether this is demonstrably true in the unique case of Shakespeare. He was far too much a disinterested craftsman ever to identify overmuch with his protagonists, though we are aware the psychoanalysts claim (absurdly, in our opinion) to the contrary. So we shall not make a composite of Shakespeare as his own tragic hero from his four great tragedies but rather content ourselves with four eternal glimpses into the dark heart of man from these incomparable tragedies, surely among the masterpieces of the whole world, though Shakespeare (to paraphrase James Russell Lowell on Edgar Allan Poe) was "two fifths sheer fudge."

For a long time, A. C. Bradley was the acknowledged master of Shakespeare (to paraphrase James Russell Lowell on Edgar Allan Poe) was "two new psychological dimension to Shakespeare and even a philosophical understanding of no common order. Of course, his cardinal error was that he continued to accept the Aristotelian idea that the tragic hero is indeed tragic precisely because he is a noble man of high estate who falls to certain doom because of *hamartia,* a fatal flaw, "a mole of nature," in his psyche, soul, self. In this tradition, critics continue to see Shakespeare's four tragic heroes as victims of a Greek *hamartia,* though, interestingly enough, it isn't *hubris,* or pride. In Hamlet, it is abulia, or the failure to act. In Macbeth, it is a consuming ambition. In King Lear, it is his excessive love for his daughters. In Othello, it is sexual jealousy.

Naturally if one accepts Aristotle's idea of *hamartia* and *catharsis,* one can read this dimension into Shakespeare; and to a certain extent it is undeniably true. Yet, as Professor Campbell has done, it is quite possible to reject the risible *hamartia* theory, which, after all, is only an ingenious theory, and to reconstruct Elizabethan psychology, in which, clearly, these four great tragic heroes are the "slaves of passions." Thereby, *Hamlet* is a tragedy of grief about melancholia. *Othello* remains a study of depression, though coupled by mania, or exaltation. *King Lear* is a tragedy of wrath in old age. By a startling metamorphosis, *Macbeth* becomes a study in fear.

We felt that, ingeniously enough, Professor Campbell substantiates her case; and her understanding of Shakespeare's tragic hero, whom we call a Christian tragic hero, assumes the novel dimension of Elizabethan psycholology, itself poles apart from the classical psychology of Aristotle. Still, there is another way to study Shakespeare, as we shall now strive to do. We postulate that Shakespeare's tragic hero is really a Christian tragic hero in a Christian context not sufficiently appreciated in current criticism of Shakespeare. As Catholic existentialists, we are superimposing upon Shakespeare a Catholic existentialism—or Anglican existentialism, since we feel that Shakespeare was truly an Anglo-Catholic (or English Catholic) in the long, incomparably rich tradition of Catholic Christianity.

Let us now begin our profile of the four great Christian tragic heroes in Shakespeare with a consideration of Hamlet. On the whole, we tend to agree with Professor Campbell rather than with Professor Bradley that "passion," as the Elizabethans understood the concept, is responsible for Hamlet's erratic behavior and ultimate downfall, for the "catastrophe" in the Greek sense of dramaturgy is clearly executed. For Hamlet was not always paralyzed by abulia, was he? He confronted the ghost, masterminded a castle conspiracy in which he pretended to be mad, and slew Polonious in a violent fit of rage. Moreover, in the dénouement, he comported himself admirably like an Elizabethan courtier, even Castiglione's own ideal courtier, acting as a warrior this time with exquisite valor. So, in a word, it is "passion," not abulia, that drives Hamlet on, as Shakespeare seems to say in the following lines:

> *What to ourselves in passion we propose,*
> *The passion ending, doth the purpose lose.*
> *The violence of either grief or joy*
> *Their own enactures with themselves destroy:*
> *Where joy most revels, grief doth most lament;*
> *Grief joys, joy grieves, on slender accident.*
>
> (*Hamlet*, III, ii, 1. 204-9)

Melancholia is the name of the passion or disorder from which Hamlet suffers, as Richard Burton admirably analyzes and depicts it in his *Anatomy of Melancholy*. Also, that passion is grief. Now, to be sure, the grief is not always debilitating, for as a Christian tragic hero Hamlet is not always so overwhelmed by abulia that he cannot make his existential option, or, so to speak, his Kierkegaardian *Sprung in die Ewigkeit*. Yet the grief is always present as the very leitmotif that explains Hamlet's essential, most innermost character: existential grief: in existential despair: with existential nausea.

In modern psychiatric terms, Hamlet has a manic-depressive psychosis, which is in itself an elaborate defense with its highs and lows against classical schizophrenia. In Professor Campbell's terminology, Hamlet is of sanguine humor, while his dramatic foil, Laertes, being of hot complexion, is of the choleric humor. Grief, or, as we prefer to call it, existential despair, gives Hamlet a keen sense of the existential thinginess, or viscosity, from which he simply cannot extricate himself from the dark heart of court affairs.

Yet, when the chips are down, we emphatically state that Hamlet, indeed, does act—effectively, too, and cogently, with his admirable existential options. For instance, in the famous scene where Hamlet sees his uncle the King praying and refuses to kill him, he fails to proceed, not through abulia, but rather because he has made an existential option to let his uncle live until he can murder him out of a state of grace and thus condemn his soul forever to perdition, surely a Catholic doctrine if there ever was one. He makes a conscious existential option for metaphysical evil, just as he opts for good (or, rather, in the Christian sense, evil) when he murders Polonius in a fit of rage and murders the King his uncle in the tragic dénouement.

Nowhere does Shakespeare describe Hamlet's manic-depressive psychosis better than in these exemplary lines:

> *So, oft it chances in particular men,*
> *That for some vicious mole of nature in them,*
> *As, in their birth—wherein they are not guilty,*
> *Since nature cannot choose his origin—*
> *By the o'ergrowth of some complexion,*
> *Oft breaking down the pales and forts of reason,*
> *Or by some habit that too much o'er-leavens*
> *The form of plausive manners, that these men,*
> *Carrying, I say, the stamp of one defect,*
> *Being nature's livery, or fortune's star,—*
> *Their virtues else—be they as pure as grace,*
> *As infinite as man may undergo—*
> *Shall in the general censure take corruption*
> *From the particular fault: the drama of eale*
> *Doth all the noble substance of a doubt*
> *To his own scandal.*
>
> (*Hamlet*, I, iv., 1. 23-37)

Now, all critics have perceived in this *hamartia,* this "mole of nature," his inability to act, his abulia: in a word, his depressive psychosis. At the same time, they rather too conveniently ignore his manic states of high elation. We readily admit that Hamlet reaches the very nadir of his depression (in grief, or existential despair) in the most famous soliloquy of all time:

> *To be, or not to be: that is the question:*
> *Whether 'tis nobler in the mind to suffer*
> *The slings and arrows of outrageous fortune,*
> *Or to take arms against a sea of troubles,*
> *And by opposing end them? To die: to sleep;*
> *No more; and by a sleep to say we end*
> *The heart-ache and the thousand natural shocks*
> *That flesh is heir to, 'tis a consummation*
> *Devoutly to be wish'd. To die, to sleep;*
> *To sleep: perchance to dream: ay, there's the rub:*
> *For in that sleep of death what dreams may come*
> *When we have shuffled off this mortal coil,*
> *Must give us pause: there's the respect*
> *That makes calamity of so long life;*
> *For who would bear the whips and scorns of time,*
> *The oppressor's wrong, the proud man's contumely,*
> *The pangs of despised love, the law's delay,*
> *The insolence of office and the spurns*
> *That patient merit of the unworthy takes,*
> *When he himself might his quietus make*
> *With a bare bodkin? who would fardels bear,*
> *To grunt and sweat under a weary life,*
> *But that the dread of something after death,*
> *The undiscover'd country from whose bourn*
> *No traveller returns, puzzles the will*
> *And makes us rather bear those ills we have*
> *Than fly to others that we know not of?*
> *Thus conscience does make cowards of us all;*
> *And thus the native hue of resolution*
> *Is sicklied o'er with the pale cast of thought,*
> *And enterprises of great pitch and moment*
> *With this regard their currents turn awry,*
> *And lose the name of action.*
>
> (*Hamlet,* III, i, 56-88)

But Hamlet is not truly suicidal, as certain critics maintain. Emphatically, he has no deathwish, as the following lines conclusively prove:

> *Love! his affections do not that way tend;*
> *Nor what he spake, though it lack'd form a little,*
> *Was not like madness. There's something in his soul*
> *O'er which his melancholy sits on brood.*
>
> (*Hamlet*, III, i, 1. 170-3)

Moreover, Hamlet, in the dénouement, flies into a manic rage in which he kills Laertes and the King. Horatio lives to tell a story that he moralizes, one that Shakespeare evidently means for his readers to accept:

> *And let me speak to the yet unknowing world*
> *How these things came about: so shall you hear*
> *Of carnal, bloody, and unnatural acts,*
> *Of accidental judgements, casual slaughters,*
> *Of deaths put on by cunning and forced cause,*
> *And, in this upshot, purposes mistook*
> *Fall'n on the inventors' heads: all this can I*
> *Truly deliver.*
>
> (*Hamlet,* Vi, ii, 1. 390-6)

At last, Hamlet welcomes death, partly from surcease of sorrow (to be sure), but also from grief, despair, abiding grief, deep grief, at the enormity of his un-Christian outrages, in which he has offended against the canon of historical Catholicism.

So, just as Professor or Bradley studied Shakespeare philosophically, and Professor Campbell psychologically, let us now come to terms with Hamlet in terms of Catholic existentialism. Like all Christian believers, Hamlet has free will, and neither God nor Satan forces him to act as he does. In a word, he, as a Catholic, is free to exercise his existential options for Christian good and not for evil. But isn't revenge sinful and essentially anti-Christian? Of course, it is. Thus, Hamlet may be a tragic hero because he is overwhelmed by a fan-shaped destiny, but at the same time he is a Christian tragic hero because he has abused the holy faith of the Mother Church in making unfortunate options for evil in evil. Hamlet, in getting his sacred revenge, has damned his eternal soul. The enormity of the tragedy of *Hamlet*, then, is that our protagonist goes so willingly to eternal perdition just to satisfy his blood-lust for revenge, surely a heinous one in Catholic Christianity. At the same time, we readers admire him for his vengefulness, and it is only with difficulty that we realize that in so doing, we have also allied ourselves with Evil in making our own wrong existential option.

As the whole world knows, *Othello* is a profound study in jealousy— and sexual jealousy at that. But what is usually forgotten is that it is a story, *de profundis*, of the sexual jealousy of a black man for a white woman in interracial love and marriage. Clearly, there is a certain ambivalence at work in this fatal relationship, almost sadomasochistic in tone and texture, in the classical study of miscegenation in English literature. It is Iago, his mortal enemy, who best characterizes Othello, the Moor of Venice, in the following lines, not only immortal verse but also perception in psychology:

> *The Moor, howbeit that I endure him not,*
> *Is of a constant, loving, noble nature,*
> *And I dare think he'll prove to Desdemona*
> *A most dear husband. Now, I do love her too;*
> *Not out of absolute lust, though peradventure*
> *I stand accountant for as great a sin,*
> *But partly led to diet my revenge,*
> *For that I do suspect the lusty Moor*
> *Hath leap'd into my seat; the thought whereof*
> *Doth, like a poisonous mineral, gnaw my inwards;*
> *And nothing can or shall content my soul*
> *Till I am even'd with him, wife for wife,*
> *Or failing so, yet that I put the Moor*
> *At least into a jealousy so strong*
> *That judgement cannot cure. Which thing to do,*
> *If this poor trash of Venice, whom I trash*
> *For his quick hunting, stand the putting on,*
> *I'll have our Michael Cassio on the hip,*
> *Abuse him to the Moor in the rank garb—*
> *For I fear Cassio with my night-cap too—*
> *Make the Moor thank me, love me and reward me,*
> *For making him egregiously an ass*
> *And practising upon his peace and quiet*
> *Even to madness. 'Tis here, but yet confused:*
> *Knavery's plain face is never seen till used.*
>   (*Othello*, II, 1, 1. 297-321)

How does the Moor, a black man desperately in love with his young white

wife, a Venetian noblewoman, though he is merely a foreigner, make his
wrong existential option, leading him ineluctably to disaster? Again, the
crux of the matter is classically pagan, right out of Greek philosophy at its
zenith in Stoicism: moderation in all matters, or, rather, the maintenance of
what Aristotle rightly called for all mankind the golden mean. But with
Othello it is the passion of sexual jealousy, which Iago carefully incites, that
distorts his reason and that ultimately leads him on in this very definition of
him as a tragic hero—and, as we shall shortly see, truly a Christian tragic
hero.

Very quickly, Iago poisons Othello's mind against the fair, charming, but
never charismatic and truly ingenuous Desdemona. Thus, we have Othello
speak of himself and Desdemona—or, rephrased, in a broad and even
metaphysical sense, of Man and Woman in their human condition:

> *O curse of marriage,*
> *That we can call these delicate creatures ours,*
> *And not their appetites! I had rather be a toad,*
> *And live upon the vapour of a dungeon,*
> *Than keep a corner in the thing I love*
> *For other's uses. Yet, 'tis the plague of great ones;*
> *Prerogatived are they less than the base;*
> *'Tis destiny unshunnable, like death:*
> *Even then this forked plague is fated to us*
> *When we do quicken.*
>
> *(Othello,* III, iii, 1. 267-78)

Iago continues to turn the knife, as the plot knots; and very soon we have
come to this point in time and space, as Othello frankly describes himself
further:

> *Had it pleased heaven*
> *To try me with affliction; had they rain'd*
> *All kinds of sores and shames on my bare head,*
> *Steep'd me in poverty to the very lips,*
> *Given to captivity me and my utmost hopes,*
> *I should have found in some place of my soul*
> *A drop of patience: but, alas, to make me*
> *A fixed figure for the time of scorn*
> *To point his slow unmoving finger at!*
> *Yet could I bear that too; well, very well:*

> *But there, where I have garner'd up my heart,*
> *Where either I must live, or bear no life;*
> *The fountain from the which my current runs,*
> *Or else dries up; to be discarded thence!*
> *Or keep it as a cistern for foul toads*
> *To knot and gender in! Turn thy complexion there,*
> *Patience, thou young and rose-lipp'd cherubin,—*
> *Ay, there, look grim as hell!*
>
> (*Othello*, IV, ili, 1. 47-64)

In the end, as a slave to the passion of sexual jealousy, Othello loses all reason—and, in a veritable moment of madness, kills the faithful but terribly naïve and ingenuous Desdemona. Shortly before the act, he realizes himself in the following lines, like a paranoiac who perceives the true nature of his very madness:

> *. . . Then must you speak*
> *Of one that love not wisely but too well;*
> *Of one not easily jealous, but being wrought*
> *Perplex'd in the extreme; of one whose hand,*
> *Like the base Indian, threw a pearl away*
> *Richer than all his tribe; of one whose subdued eyes,*
> *Albeit unused to the melting mood,*
> *Drop tears as fast as the Arabian trees*
> *Their medicinal gum. Set you down this;*
> *And say besides, that in Aleppo once,*
> *Where a malignant and a turban'd Turk*
> *Beat a Venetian and traduced the state,*
> *I took by the throat the circumcised dog,*
> *And smote him, thus.*
>
> (*Othello*, V, ii, 1. 343-56)

What are the results of this madness, this loss of reason to Elizabethan "passion"? Brabantio dies from the grief over the marriage of his fair daughter. Roderigo dies through a "just retribution" that comes to him as a result of his "unholy love." Emilia dies through the angry vengeance of her husband. Desdemona is unjustly murdered as Othello, our slave of passion, tries to avenge his sense of honor. Othello commits suicide in his own final grief, or existential despair, in his existential nausea, for having made the wrong existential option. Iago awaits his punishment.

Certainly, Othello comes to high tragedy because, as Bradley says, he has a *hamartia*, and because, as Campbell argues, he is a "slave of passion." Both points of view are true—as far as they define the intensity of Othello's metaphysical suffering as a tragic hero. But our own point of view, as Catholic critics, is that Othello assumes an added dimension as "a Christian tragic hero" precisely through his failure as a Christian to make the right existential options.

For is it not certain that the Christian takes, or should take, his greatest joy in life by making existential options that root him in *koinonia* with *caritas* and lead him inevitably and even ineluctably ever closer to God in his quest for salvation? We think so. What did the Old Testament prophet Hosea do with his unfaithful wife? He continued to love her, and though not a Christian, Hosea acted admirably well. What did the Stoic emperor Marcus Aruelius do with his whore of a wife, Faustina? He continued to love her, and though a Stoic and an anti-Christian, he acted admirably.

Likewise, Othello should not have given way to his "passion" of sexual jealousy. He should have kept his classical reason, also profoundly a Christian reason. He should have opted for the Christian virtues of forgiveness and of love within a Christian marriage, itself a blessed sacrament of the Holy Church. But he did none of this. Instead, he opted for evil. Therefore, in the end, though we admire Othello and fully empathize with him and suffer with him in the texture of his own metaphysical suffering, we must admit that above all, he is a "Christian tragic hero" because in the end he acted evilly, opting for evil in a Christian cosmos in which we all, as Christians, have a God-given free will that we must kinetically exert to bring us ever closer to our apprehension of God and not away from him for the religious night of the World, the Flesh, and the Devil. This, in summary, is Shakespeare's profoundly Christian message—and properly defines Shakespeare as a great Christian writer, though his Christianity is only implicit and not explicit in the great tragedy of *Othello*.

Now, we come to a careful consideration of *Macbeth*. Like Professor Bradley, nearly all modern critics have interpreted this singular tragedy as a classical study of overwhelming ambition. Professor Campbell, however, does not concur. Rather, she sees Macbeth as a slave of passion who, in the end, represents the debilitating effect of fear. This position is not at all so preposterous as it at first seems. Indeed, there is more than a kernel of truth in it.

Yet these positions are not nearly so antithetical as one may at first assume. Both ideas are totally correct. We intend to reconcile them by making an existentialist hero *manqué* of Macbeth, also a Christian tragic hero.

as he consciously and self-consciously opts for evil in cruel ambition, though also sometimes in abulia from fear, or, as the Germans would more properly and denotatively say, and as we think Professor Campbell truly means, with *Angst.*

What is the relation of action, motivated by ambition, to fear? Even the hare, when cornered, will put up a hell of a fight. In a word, Macbeth, in the tragedy, was cornered: by the witches, by his wife, by his ambition itself. All the while, he felt great fear—and abulia in and from that fear, for clearly he is something of a neurasthenic, while Hamlet is a manic-depressive type. In truth, then, he lashes out savagely, even sadistically, in murderous fear. This is the true explanation of his personality; and this is why, though he is a Christian tragic hero, he is also something of an existentialiste manqué.

These lines, at once, relate his ambition to his fear, as he hesitates at the tempting thought of making an existential option for murder, i.e., evil:

> *This supernatural soliciting*
> *Cannot be ill, cannot be good: if ill,*
> *Why hath it given me earnest of success,*
> *Commencing in a truth? I am thane of Cawdor:*
> *If good, why do I yield to that suggestion*
> *Whose horrid image doth unfix my hair*
> *And make my seated heart knock at my ribs,*
> *Against the use of nature? Present fears*
> *Are less than horrible imaginings:*
> *My thought, whose murder yet is but fantastical,*
> *Shakes so my single state of man that function*
> *Is smother'd in surmise, and nothing is*
> *But what is not.*
>
> (*Macbeth,* I, iii, 1. 130-42)

The meaning is implicit. We cannot fail to apprehend its message in the evident psychology of Macbeth.

Lady Macbeth is the temptress as she catalyzes her husband, tries to galvanize him into action: an existential option, in the following lines, that relates fear (and also nobility) to the dominant motif of ambition:

> *What thou art promised: yet do I fear thy nature;*
> *It is too full o' the milk of human kindness*
> *To catch the nearest way: thou wouldst be great;*
> *Art not without ambition, but without*

> *The illness should attend it: what thou couldst highly,*
> *Thou wouldst holily; wouldst not play false,*
> *And yet wouldst wrongly win: thou 'ldst have, great Glamis,*
> *That which rather thou dost fear to do*
> *Than wishest should be undone.' Hie thee hither,*
> *That I may pour my spirits in thine ear;*
> *And chastise with the valour of my tongue*
> *All that impedes thee from the golden round,*
> *Which fate and metaphysical aid doth seem*
> *To have thee crown'd withal.*
>
> (*Macbeth*, I, v, 1. 17-31)

At first, Macbeth wavers. Consumed by ambition, gnawed in his vitals by fear (the Furies, or Erinyes of Greek thought), he, at last, makes his existential option to kill for the savage sake of his ambition:

> *If it were done when 'tis done, then 'twere well*
> *It were done quickly: if the assassination*
> *Could trammel up the consequence, and catch*
> *With his surcease success; that but this blow*
> *Might be the be-all and the end-all here,*
> *But here, upon this bank and shoal of time,*
> *We'ld jump the life to come. But in these cases*
> *We still have judgement here; that we but teach*
> *Bloody instructions, which, being taught, return*
> *To plague the inventor: this even handed justice*
> *Commends the ingredients of our poison'd chalice*
> *To our own lips.*
>
> (*Macbeth*, I, vii, 1. 1-12)

These are powerful lines. Macbeth, then executes his existential option, his heart knocking against his ribs, as desperately (in great fear) he lashes himself on into furious actions.

Once Macbeth opts for evil, he must follow his bloody road to the bitter end—and mires up more and more deeply in the existential thinginess of metaphysical evil. He is consumed by ambition, as Professor Bradley says. He is also consumed by fear, as Professor Campbell argues. These lines accurately depict the sad state of his shattered Christian psyche, self, soul:

> *To be thus is nothing;*
> *But to be safely thus.—Our fears in Banquo*

Stick deep; and in his royalty of nature
Reigns that which would be fear'd: 'tis much he dares;
And, to that dauntless temper of his mind,
He hath a wisdom that doth guide his valour
To act in safety. There is none but he
Whose being I do fear: and, under him,
My genius is rebuked; as, it is said,
Mark Antony's was by Caesar.

(Macbeth, III, i, 1. 48-57)

Again, he opts for evil. Again, it is fear that motivates him even more than his ambition. Banquo is murdered, though Fleance escapes.

Macbeth suffers Christian guilt. He sees apparitions. In the famous banquet scene, he sees the apparition of the murdered Banquo, though Lady Macbeth analyzes it thusly:

O proper stuff!
This is the very painting of your fear:
This is the air-drawn dagger which, you said,
Led you to Duncan. O, these flaws and starts,
Imposters to true fear, would well become
A woman's story at a winter's fire,
Authorized by her grandam. Shame itself!
Why do you make such faces? When all's done,
You look but on a stool.

(Macbeth, III, iv., 1. 60-68)

She says "fear," and means "fear," and certainly "fear" it is; Professor Campbell is more perceptive than the now canonized Professor Bradley, At this point, consumed by his fear, Macbeth falls into the cold sweat of his abulia—and is psychologically unable, at least for the moment, to make further existential options.

Yet Professor Campbell comes to a point of diminishing returns as she stresses her remarkable "fear theory." The world is kinetic, as the existentialists well know; we are all constantly changing, developing, even metamorphosing. The moment comes when, as he says of himself, analyzing himself, Macbeth, steeped in blood, has lost all intimations of fear and its effects in abulia:

I have almost forgot the taste of fears:
The time has been, my senses would have cool'd

> *To hear a night-shriek; and my fell of hair*
> *Would at a dismal treatise rouse and stir*
> *As life were in 't: I have supp'd full with horrors;*
> *Direness, familiar to my slaughterous thoughts,*
> *Cannot once start me.*
>
> (Macbeth, V, v, 1. 8-15)

Macduff, his great adversary, "not born of woman," and thus fatal to Macbeth, is emphatically on the march. Presciently, Macbeth suspects the worst and intuits impending disaster, ultimate doom. Brilliantly, he dissects himself in a spot of time and in a certain place thusly:

> *I will not yield,*
> *To kiss the ground before young Malcolm's feet,*
> *And to be baited with the rabble's curse.*
> *Though Birnam Wood be come to Dunsinane,*
> *And thou opposed, being of no woman born,*
> *Yet I will try the last. Before my body*
> *I throw my warlike shield. Lay on, Macduff,*
> *And damn'd be him that first cries "Hold, enough!"*
>
> (Macbeth, V, viii, 1. 27-34)

Undaunted, knowing he is to die, knowing he will spend eternity in hell for his vile murders, Macbeth, in the dénouement, in the sword fight with Macduff, speaks thusly, as he makes his final existential option for bravery, which seems to refute or attenuate Professor Campbell's rather dogmatic insistence on fear as the leitmotif of Macbeth.

In her conclusion, Professor Campbell sees rashness as the other side of the coin to fear. We cannot quite agree, though we see her point of view. Surely, our quotations show Macbeth as a cold analyst of his own passions and a man of incredible sangfroid in his cruel ambition. Hence, we maintain that the key to Macbeth's character is not ambition, as Professor Bradley maintains, or fear-rashness, as Professor Campbell maintains, but rather his troubled conscience as a Christian tragic hero aware of his own singular imperfections. For, essentially, the tragedy, at least in a spiritual sense, is that Macbeth has been a good Christian, a noble man, a great warrior, who, once opting for evil, pursues Evil to the very point of his eternal damnation. And in our Christian cosmos is there any greater tragedy than the damnation of a once mighty soul in the service of our Risen Lord?

Traditionally, Shakespearean critics have understood *King Lear* as the tragedy of a senile old man who is too loving, too magnanimous, far too generous with his three daughters, two of whom regard him as a bovine old fool. This is certainly a limited point of view. Rightly, Professor Campbell sees in King Lear the added dimension of "wrath in old age." Certainly, she is correct in her cogent analysis. King Lear fumes and splutters impotently throughout the play as a very wrathful old man. Once again, however, we interpret his behavior in terms of Christian and even Catholic existentialism.

We get a first glimpse into the rashness and irascibility of King Lear when he lashes out against his daughter Cordelia for her tempered speech about how deeply she loves her doting old father:

> *Let it be so; thy truth, then, be thy dower.*
> *For, by the sacred radiance of the sun,*
> *The mysteries of Hecate, and the night;*
> *By all the operation of the orbs*
> *From whom we do exist, and cease to be;*
> *Here I disclaim all my paternal care,*
> *Propinquity and property of blood,*
> *And as a stranger to my heart and me*
> *Hold thee, from this, forever. The barbarous Scythian,*
> *Or he that makes his generation messes*
> *To gorge his appetite, shall to my bosom*
> *Be as well neighbour'd, pitied, and relieved,*
> *As thou my sometime daughter.*
>
> (*King Lear*, I, i, 1. 110-22)

King Lear, in these lines, has made his first existential option in *mauvaise foi* (bad faith) as the thinginess, or viscosity, of the World, the Flesh, and the Devil closes in upon him. From this point on, we begin our certain descent into assured tragedy, breathtakingly beautiful and poignant, breathtakingly fearful and damning.

Goneril and Regan, his other two daughters, soon sell out their overly generous (and thus sucker) father. Heartlessly, they turn him out into the wild night, as Goneril says, because:

> *By day and night he wrongs me; every hour*
> *He flashes into one gross crime or other,*
> *That sets us all at odds: I'll not endure it:*
> *His knights grow riotous, and himself upbraids us*
> *On every trifle. When he returns from hunting,*

> *I will not speak with him; say I am sick:*
> *If you come slack of former services,*
> *You shall do well; the fault of it I'll answer.*
>
> > *(King Lear*, I, iii, 1. 3-7)

After this fatal confrontation, King Lear has his moment of self-encounter in a rare moment of truth laid bare. Impotently, he strikes back as best he can. He stalks out with his fool (jester) into the blue and wild night.

King Lear, as he knows, as he admits, borders on madness:

> *O, let met not be mad, not mad, sweet heaven!*
> *Keep me in temper: I would not be mad!*
>
> > *(King Lear*, I, v, 1. 50-51)

But it would be wrong to think he ever steps into madness. Later, his wrath, as his Elizabethan passion, degenerates into sheer impotence, as the following lines indicate:

> *You see me here, you gods, a poor old man,*
> *As full of grief as age; wretched in both!*
> *If it be you that stir these daughters' hearts*
> *Against their father, fool me not so much*
> *To bear it tamely; touch me with noble anger,*
> *And let not women's weapons, water-drops,*
> *Stain my man's cheeks! No, you unnatural hags,*
> *I will have such revenges on you both,*
> *That all the world shall—I will do such things,—*
> *What they are, yet I know not; but they shall be*
> *The terrors of the earth.*
>
> > *(King Lear*, II, iv, 1. 275-85)

While he runs the gamut of all the passion in this speech, it is impotence with a hint of salivating senility that we most intuit.

Shakespeare himself seems to agree with Professor Campbell more than with Professor Bradley, in the speech when the doctor explains to Cordelia, as King Lear is brought on the stage to be awakened after his healing sleep:

> *Be comforted, good madam: the great rage,*
> *You see, is kill'd in him: and yet it is danger*

To make him even o'er the time he has lost.
Desire him to go in; trouble him no more
Till further settling.

(King Lear, IV, vii, 1. 78-83)

In the dénouement, Lear enters, bearing the body of his now beloved Cordelia, the faithful and loving daughter, whom he has greatly wronged. After this, Lear will be mad forever, as in a Christian sense he pays for, or atones for, the metaphysical crime he has committed against filial love in the form of his daughter. He dies in pitiful madness as a release from his terrible suffering.

Surely, *King Lear* is all these things at once: a study of magnanimity and generosity, of old age, of senility, certainly of wrath, as Professor Campbell rightly argues in her analysis of this Elizabethan passion. Most relevant to our age, however, is the existentialist element. As a Christian, King Lear makes the wrong existential options in the bad faith of his nausea–and thus becomes a tragic Christian hero. For he cannot live his faith, and is there a worse tragedy for the Christian, whose loss of faith means wrong choice and, from wrong choice, eternal damnation?

We wish to make two concluding statements, both of which may startle and challenge the very holy canon of Shakespeareana.

Enigmatically, there is a sense in which Shakespeare is the king of all frivolous writers. Despite his psychological depth and philosophical breadth, we do not think he regarded himself with the high seriousness with which Christopher Marlowe and Ben Jonson so apparently did. Mostly, Shakespeare was a skilled craftsman and wanted to turn a fast dollar on the London stage. In this sense, he was very much like a Hollywood playwright. At his worst, in this light, Shakespeare was an Alfred Hitchcock turning out amusing and even engrossing trivia (gold bricks) for our amusement. At his best, he was the equivalent of the great British playwright, Robert Bolt, a man of incredible gifts and great insight, whose *Lawrence of Arabia* (in a cinéma sense) is the equivalent of *Othello*. Now the language is different, since the conditions have changed. But our point is instructive. If Shakespeare were alive today, he would undoubtedly write for the mass market of the cinéma, and he would probably be very much like Robert Bolt most of the time. And while we would admire him less, we would love him even more; for the essential name of the game with Bolt and Shakespeare is ever amusement: not really *plaire et instruire,* but really just *plaire.*

Enigmatically, too, there is another sense in which Shakespeare is our most serious writer–and our greatest: the Christian sense, though this is the very facet of Shakespeare that has been least studied and needs most to be studied. Now, Shakespeare is not explicitly Christian, and we must make the effort to apprehend his truly Christian message. But his essential Christianity is there in the humanistic mold, a fabulous treasure that has never been explored to date. We have superficially analyzed him as a Christian existentialist, even a Catholic existentialist. But this is merely a pilot study, and we leave it to others to analyze and synthesize the warm, vibrant, vital Christianity of Shakespeare. For Shakespeare is under attack, not from scholars and professional students but rather from the mass public of the English-speaking people to whom he is a forbidding figure, no longer relevant to our times. To retain Shakespeare, we must humanize him: Christianize him. To humanize him, we must analyze his Christian tragic heroes and then synthesize them into a composite of the incomparable Christian tragic hero that William Shakespeare of Stratford-on-Avon and the Globe Theater so triumphantly is: a saint among men and thus a legend of godliness and goodness in his own time, for our times, and for all times, for all men everywhere.

Milton as Christian Tragic Hero

There have been a number of excellent studies that touch upon or treat the Miltonic hero. .E.M.W. Tillyard's *Milton* and *Studies in Milton* come to mind. John M. Steadman published his admirable *Milton and the Renaissance Hero* in 1967. Edward Wagenknecht's *The Personality of Milton* is somewhat less satisfactory, since he seems to have several critical axes to grind, especially the anti-romantic bias against Satan as the hero of *Paradise Lost* and *Paradise Regained*.

In general, Professor Wagenknecht typifies contemporary American reaction to Milton, while Professor Tillyard represents British and European opinion. On the whole, we find ourselves far more in agreement with Professor Tillyard than with Professor Wagenknecht, on the role of Satan as the prototype of the Miltonic hero, as the Europeans still perceive him (following the English romantics Blake and Shelley), though Professor Wagenknecht inexactly claims this "myth" was exploded long ago. Moreover, Professor Wagenknecht's work is far more "popular" and far less academic than that of Professor Tillyard.

It is Professor Steadman who, in recent years, most explicitly treats the problem of the Miltonic hero, himself a *porte-parole* of Milton both as poet and man of action. Professor Steadman, an admirable scholar, has thoroughly documented the case for the Miltonic hero's being a Renaissance hero: documented it, to the point that this otherwise exemplary study is for the most part a *catalogue raisonné* of literary allusions and references: encyclopedic, to be sure, but quite limited in the aesthetic, psychological, philosophical, and religious perceptions of the Miltonic hero precisely because it lacks a keen and original critical insight.

Still, within its limits, Professor Steadman's book is the best ever written on the topic of the hero. If he errs in this study at all, it is by omitting the medieval and Romantic dimensions of Milton's work and mind. Thus, we should like to analyze the Christian tragic hero in Milton (or "the Miltonic hero," as it has been traditionally and somewhat inexactly called) in the three dimensions of the medieval Everyman, the Renaissance courtier ("hero"), and the Romantic hero. For we claim that Milton has religious roots in the Middle Ages, faces the recent Renaissance in the England of his day, and foreshadows the Romantic revolution of the early nineteenth century. In this context, we shall limit ourselves to a consideration of *Paradise Lost, Paradise Regained,* and *Samson Agonistes,* since together they denote the archetypal hero in Milton's mind and work.

As Professor Tillyard points out in "The Crisis of *Paradise Lost*" from his *Studies in Milton,* Adam is as much the hero of the epic as Satan in the sense that, as if from the Middle Ages, he is Everyman on his quest for salvation. To the extent that Adam is a medieval figure, this observation is emphatically true. But to the point that Adam is a Renaissance courtier, it is only partially true, since Satan is clearly more the prototype of the Renaissance courtier, or "ideal man," or "hero." And in the sense that Adam and Satan are both Romantic heroes, it is emphatically Satan who, as Blake and Shelley first observed—and rightly, too—was the great hero precisely because he evidenced all the qualities of "titanism" enumerated by Professor Steadman: (1) fortitude; (2) sapience; (3) leadership; (4) *amor* (self-love, or egoism); and (5) magnanimity. He neglected to allude to the all-important Nietzschean will to power in the Renaissance and Romantic, are also present in Christ and Samson Agonistes. Hence, as we can see, there are three historical (and thus philosophical and religious) dimensions to the protagonists of these three great poems, *Paradise Lost, Paradise Regained,* and *Samson Agonistes.*

The Everyman motif in Book I of *Paradise Lose* has often been noted:

> *. . . What in me is dark*
> *Illumine, what is low raise and support;*
> *That to the highth of this great argument*
> *I may assert Eternal Providence*
> *And justify the ways of God to men.*

(1. 22-26)

In a sense, Adam, as the protagonist, is Everyman. In a sense, too, by extension, it is every Christian believer who follows him in time and space, including Milton, by implication, since *Paradise Lost* (in a poetic sense) is the "genesis" of the pilgrimage of man, which Everyman, indeed, has undertaken for the sake of his immortal soul. Adam, of course, is Man, Everyman, who at first seems to accept willingly enough God's one prohibition to him and his beloved spouse, Eve:

> ... *"Then let us not think hard*
> *One easy prohibition, who enjoy*
> *Full leave so large to all things else, and choice*
> *Unlimited of manifold delights;*
> *But let us ever praise him, and extol*
> *His bounty, following our delightful task*
> *To prune these growing plants, and tend these flow'rs,*
> *Which were it toilsome, yet with thee were sweet."*
>
> (Book IV, 1. 432-39)

From these words, it appears immediately that Adam is bovine and uxorious: something of an insufferable ass, quite less than heroic. Is Everyman any different, or is the Christian tragic hero, for are they not an expression of man's basic weaknesses, themselves "certain infirmities of the soul?" Eve, the distaff side of Everyman, is as vain and domineering and bossy and frivolous as modern masochists like to say of the Modern Woman, reflecting upon her own image:

> ... *"What thou seest*
> *What there thou seest, fair creature, is thyself,*
> *With thee it came and goes; but follow me,*
> *And I will bring thee where no shadow stays*
> *Thy coming, and thy soft embraces, he*
> *Whose image thou art, him thou shalt enjoy*
> *Inseparably thine; to him shalt bear*
> *Multitudes like thyself, and thence be called*
> *Mother of human race."*
>
> (Book IV, 1. 467-75)

Thus, immediately, Milton posits "natural process" between man and woman in a common quest for salvation, then within the Garden of Eden, but so soon afterward in the world, pinioned between Flesh and the Devil. The portraits, of course, are one-dimensional stereotypes, simplistic in nature and perhaps by design. For though a powerful poet, Milton was an incredibly weak psychologist, who never apprehended the real nature of man and woman, *de profundis*, as Dante, Baudelaire, and T.S. Eliot, among other religious writers, always did.

As Adam (Everyman) kisses Eve (the Eternally Feminine, as Goethe might well have called her), Milton describes Satan in the simplistic terms of the silent cinéma screen, *circa* the Great War, when the evil proprietor tries to evict the penniless widow from her hovel, as he twirls his mustachioes with a diabolical leer and sensual smirk:

> *. . . Aside the Devil turned*
> *For envy, yet with jealous leer malign*
> *Eyed them askance, and to himself thus plained. . . .*
>
> (Book IV, 1. 502-4)

Adam and Eve are both obtuse, heedless of the dark future. But was not Everyman, too, in the medieval morality play? Satan alone has any of the Renaissance qualities that, erroneously, Professor Steadman professed to have found in Adam. Moreover, Satan, in the romantic guise, has a Herculean and also Nietzschean will to power in the best nineteenth-century tradition. In the Garden of Eden, as Milton so simplistically (and thus so Puritanically) delineates it, Adam and Eve both have their sensibilities stifled by an insensitive God who might very well have stepped from the more lurid pages of Lautréamont's epic, *Les Chants de Maldoror:* Jehovah bites Adam's head off for presuming to certain questions just as surely as Lautréamont's God bites off babies' heads (and belches with his supreme pleasure) upon his throne of human bones.

The one-dimensional psychology, almost that of risible caricatures, certainly of stereotypes, even for Milton's religiously unsophisticated times, continues with convenient tags around Satan, e.g., the "Arch Fiend." We suppose that, as if in a nickleodeon in 1920, we are supposed to boo and hiss when the Arch Fiend appears, just as we are supposed to applaud and cheer at the appearance of "virtuous" Adam and "guileless' Eve.

Finally, however, the evil serpent has his way in a blatant temptation scene that ill compares with the sophisticated subtleties of, say, Gustave Flaubert in his poetic and imagistic *La Tentation de Saint Antoine.* Thus, Milton writes succinctly, though perhaps not succinctly enough:

> *So saying, her rash hand in evil hour*
> *For the reaching to the fruit, she plucked, she eat.*
> *Earth felt the wound, and Nature from her seat*
> *Sighing through all her works gave signs of woe,*
> *That all was lost. Back to the thicket slunk*
> *The guilty Serpent, and well might, for Eve*
> *Intent now wholly on her taste, naught else*

Regarded; such delight till then, as seemed,
In fruit she never tasted, whether true
Or fancies so, nor was Godhead from her thought.
Greedily she engorged without restraint,
And knew not eating death. Satiate at length,
And heightened as with wine, jocund and boon,
Thus to herself she pleasingly began.

(Book IX, 1. 780-94)

After eating the apple (or "peach," as it seems to have been), she "gave the core" to Adam, who ingested it uxoriously so that, nobly (or was it "masochistically?"), he would always be with Eve in her damnation. Milton concludes this sober scene with much heady rhetroic and all the psychology of a thirteen-year-old boy who has just discovered the anatomical difference between boys and girls:

To whom then first incensed Adam replied:
"Is this the love, is this the recompense
Of mine to thee, ingrateful Eve, expressed
Inscrutable when thou wast lost, not I,
Who might have lived and joyed immortal bliss,
Yet willingly chose rather death with thee?
And am I now upbraided, as the case
Of thy transgressing? Not enough severe,
It seems, in thy restraint. What could I more?
I warned thee, I admonished thee, foretold
The danger, and the lurking enemy
That lay in wait; beyond this had been force,
And force upon free will hath here no place.
But confidence then bore thee on, secure
Either to meet no danger, or to find
Matter of glorious trial; and perhaps
I also erred in overmuch admiring
What seemed in thee so perfect, that I thought
No evil durst attempt thee, but I rue
That error now, which is become my crime,
And thou th'accuser. Thus it shall befall
Him who to worth in women overtrusting
Lets her will rule; restraint she will not brook,
And left to herself, if evil thence ensue,

> *She first his weak indulgence will accuse."*
>   *Thus they in mutual accusation spent*
> *The fruitless hours, but neither self-condemning,*
> *And of their vain contest appeared no end.*
>
> (Book IX, 1. 1162-89)

The concluding lines are psychologically specious. The amateur psychologist, as was Milton, who knew nothing of the human heart, though he had fathomed the grandeur of suffering (in which Greek "pain" becomes "gain"), would say that they accused each other, not themselves: accused each other, yes, especially at first, but later beat their own breasts too, most bitterly, as subtle religious poets like Dante Alighieri, Charles Baudeliare, T.S. Eliot, and Paul Claudel would surely point out for their protagonists' scarlet consciousness of sin and guilt, always delicious (almost suppurating for its exquisite *faisandage*) in its sadomasochistic dimensions.

Free will was important for Milton in his theology, as we well know, perhaps because it figured so heavily in the religious thought of the time, but perhaps also because it was the *élan vital*, or motor force, of the Renaissance hero, thus a concept doubly important in the dimensions of our Christian tragic hero. In this light, tagging poor Satan again, Milton writes one-dimensionally:

> *Meanwhile at heinous and despiteful act*
> *Of Satan done in Paradise, and how*
> *He in the Serpent had perverted Eve,*
> *Her husband she, to taste the fatal fruit,*
> *Was known in heav'n; for what can scape the eye*
> *Of God all-seeing, or deceive his heart*
> *Omniscient, who in all things wise and just,*
> *Hindered not Satan to attempt the mind*
> *Of man, with strength entire, and free will armed,*
> *Complete to have discovered the repulsed*
> *Whatever wiles of woe or seeming friend?*
> *For still they knew, and ought to have still remembered,*
> *The high injunction not to taste that fruit,*
> *Whoever tempted; which they not obeying,*
> *Incurred (what could they less) the penalty,*
> *And manifold in sin, deserved to fall.*
>
> (Book X, 1. 1-16)

Thus, to Milton's mind, and as the Bible would say, the wages of sin is death;

and, in truth, death has now entered the Garden of Eden, Paradise, now metamorphosed into the arena of the World, the Flesh, and the Devil. Still, Milton, as a Christian, thus as his own tragic hero, is concerned with redemptive grace, and he concludes Book X in this guise about Adam and Eve:

> *So spake our father penitent, nor Eve*
> *Felt less remorse. They forthwith to the place*
> *Repairing where he judged them, prostrate fell*
> *Before him reverent, and both confessed*
> *Humbly their faults, and pardon begged, with tears*
> *Watering the ground, and with their sighs the air*
> *Frequenting, sent from hearts contrite, in sign*
> *Of sorrow unfeigned, and humiliation meek.*
>
> (Book X, 1. 1097-1104)

The poetry is magnificent, barreled out in the dulcet tones of Wordsworth's "organ voice" depiction of Milton at his best. Yet the psychology is only passable. The theology would never satisfy a contemporary thinker, whether Fundamentalist or existentialist.

Here, too, with a keen and cutting consciousness of guilt, they begin their quest for salvation, as Everyman, in the best medieval tradition of the morality play. It is God who presents his son, Jesus Christ, the Messiah, who intercedes for them in his eternal design for salvation. A Homeric catalog explains the geographical dimensions of Adam's journey through time and space, at least through his numberless descendants:

> *To whom thus Adam gratefully replied;*
> *"Ascend, I follow thee, safe guide, the path*
> *Thou leads't me, and to the hand of Heaven submit,*
> *However chast'ning, to the evil turn*
> *My obvious breast, arming to overcome*
> *By suffering, and earn rest from labor won,*
> *If so I may attain." So both ascend*
> *In the visions of God. It was a hill*
> *Of Paradise the highest, from whose top*
> *The hemisphere of earth in clearest ken*
> *Stretched out to amplest reach of prospect lay.*
> *Not higher that hill nor wider looking round,*
> *Whereon for different cause the Tempter set*
> *Our second Adam in the wilderness,*

> *To show him all earth's kindgoms and their glory.*
>   (Book XI, 1. 379-384)

The ensuing catalogue is well worthy of Homer. Also, the Archangel Michael shows the distraught Adam prescient glimpses of the ineluctable future in which man, in his spiritual quest, works out a salvation made efficacious for him by the Messiah through his death, as foreshadowed in Book XIII. Book XI concludes, then, on the following somber note:

> *To whom th'Archangel: "Dextrously thou aim'st;*
> *So willingly doth God remit his ire,*
> *Though late repenting him of man depraved,*
> *Grieved at his heart, when looking down he saw*
> *The whole earth filled with violence, and all flesh*
> *Corrupting each their way; yet those removed,*
> *Such grace shall one just man find in his sight,*
> *That he relents, not to blot out mankind,*
> *And makes a covenant never to destroy*
> *The earth again by flood, nor let the sea*
> *Surpass his bounds, nor rain to drown the world*
> *With man therein or beast; but when he brings*
> *Over the earth a cloud, will therein set*
> *His triple-colored bow, whereon to look*
> *And call to mind his covenant. Day and night,*
> *Seed-time and harvest, till fire purge all things new,*
> *Both heav'n and earth, wherein the just shall dwell."*
>   (Book XI, 884-901)

Milton's worldview is indeed simplistic, as if it came out of the Scofield Bible, in which the world (ostensibly) began in 4004 B.C. on September 1 at nine o'clock in the morning. Of course, it may be argued that at this time nearly everybody accepted the naïve Biblical account of creation; but the point is that the sophisticates did not and do not. Lucretius' *De Rerum naturae*, with its explicit theory of evolution, had been in the canon of Western culture for some sixteen hundred years. Milton, if he truly believed in free will, didn't have merely to summarize the world view of his age. With his magnificent intellect, truly a catholic intellect, he could well have foreshadowed the New Science—and, indeed, the theology of "demythologization" of Rudolf Bultmann. For this, we blame Milton: for the certain measure of his simplistic religiosity.

Finally, at the end of Book XII, Adam and Eve, as the male and female (the old lingam-yoni principle?) aspects of Everyman, come to the end of their quest, itself the new beginning, as they are formally expelled from the Garden of Eden:

> *To whom thus also th'Angel last replied:*
> *"This having learnt, thou hast attained the sum*
> *Of wisdom; hope no higher, though all the stars*
> *Thou knew'st by name, and all th'ethereal powers,*
> *All secrets of the deep, all Nature's works,*
> *Or works of God in heav'n, air, earth, or sea,*
> *And all the riches of this world enjoy'dst.*
> *And all the rule, one empire; only add*
> *Deeds to thy knowledge answerable, add faith,*
> *Add virtue, patience, temperance, add love,*
> *By name to come called charity, the soul*
> *Of all the rest: then wilt thou not be loth*
> *To leave this Paradise, but shalt possess*
> *A paradise within thee, happier far.*
> *Let us descend now therefore from this top*
> *Of speculation; for the hour precise*
> *Exacts our parting hence; and see the guards,*
> *By me encamped on yonder hill, expect*
> *Their motion, at whose front a flaming sword,*
> *In signal of remove, waves fiercely round;*
> *We may no longer stay: go, waken Eve;*
> *Her also I with gentle dreams have calmed,*
> *Portending good, and all her spirits composed*
> *To meek submission: thou at season fit*
> *Let her with thee partake what thou hast heard,*
> *Chiefly what may concern her faith to know,*
> *The great deliverance by her seed to come*
> *(For by the Woman's Seed) on all mankind:*
> *That ye may live, which will be many days,*
> *Both in one faith unanimous though sad,*
> *With cause for evils past, yet much more cheered*
> *With meditation on the happy end."*
> (Book XII, 1. 574-605)

Brilliantly enough, *Paradise Lost* ends on an open note, that is, for the New

Beginning (the pursuit of the religious quest) that will have no metaphysical ending till the Second Coming of Christ. Milton, here as elsewhere, is a brilliant orchestrator; he well manipulates the calculated effect within the context of the literary epic. Wordsworth was right to refer to Milton's "great organ voice," which, in its highly Latinate poetry, in the baroque manner, was never surpassed. As with James Joyce in prose, Milton has a more complete mastery of the English language than any other writer, not excluding the luminaries of Shakespeare, Chaucer, Spenser, Marlowe, the translators of the King James Bible, and the authors of the *Book of Common Prayer.* Yet, do his simplistic theology and his paper-thin psychology really serve him well; or are they, rather, what has alienated Eliot and his literary adherents? Emphatically, we think so. But since the subject of our essay is simply Milton as Christian tragic hero, let us summarize what we have said so far.

Adam and Eve are Everyman, but they are questionably not the Renaissance heroes whom Professor Steadman tries vainly to find in them, albeit with much documentation. Is Adam the prototype of Castiglione's ideal courtier, i.e., the Renaissance hero? We think not. He is neither a poet nor a philosopher; he is neither a warrior nor a scientist; he is neither sophisticated nor witty; he is not even polished, "finished" in the Renaissance sense. Indeed, he is an uxorious, bovine ass. Eve, for her part, is domineering, frivolous, and bitchy, the very prototype of the modern American white woman in the eyes of the Europeans and the Third Worlders. Furthermore, Adam and Eve lack the titanism and sensibility to foreshadow the Romantic hero and heroine of the nineteenth century.

What are we left with? Satan! Despite contemporary American antagonism to this point of view, as Professor Wagenknecht tries vainly to substantiate, we can only conclude with Shelley and Blake that Satan is indeed the real tragic hero (a Christian *manqué,* or *à rebours*) of *Paradise Lost.* To be sure, he is not Everyman on a spiritual quest. Yet he is emphatically a Renaissance hero, since he possesses the many desirable facets of the Renaissance courtier—and, at times, even has a dry, acerbic wit. Moreover, he foreshadows the titanism, the disoriented sensibility, the effusive psychology, and the Nietzschean will to power of the Romantic hero, as seen most readily in Lord Byron's Manfred. We regret that literary criticism is subject to vogues, that now the American tendency is to neglect the heroic aspects of Satan, that many forget (as seems most obvious with us) that Satan (with all his martial pomp and administrative genius) is the only dramatically satisfactory protagonist of *Paradise Lost,* and that Milton's unconscious sympathies were clearly with him, as ours consciously are in his struggle against an adamant God.

Now we come to *Paradise Regained,* a noble failure from the dramatic point of view if there ever was one, since the poem lacks ultimate impact and since few of us can identify very much with Christ as the hero. But at the outset Milton states his thesis, which, expounded, will develop into the four books of well-orchestrated poetic effect:

> *I who erewhile the happy garden sung,*
> *By one man's disobedience lost, now sing*
> *Recovered Paradise to all mankind,*
> *By one man's firm obedience fully tried*
> *Through all temptation, and the Tempter foiled*
> *In all his wiles, defeated and repulsed,*
> *And Eden raised in the waste wilderness.*
> *(Book I, 1. 1-7)*

Clearly, the hero of the poem is Jesus, the perfect man, yet more than man, too, as God in the Flesh. Certainly, it is difficult for us with our singular imperfections to empathize with God. Moreover, we are reminded of the old American Western films, when the hero wore a white hat and the villain a black hat. Emphatically, Christ, as we would suspect, is cloaked in white with all but a golden halo, making him too imperial and forbidding for our readers' sympathies. Satan, once again, is the arch-fiend, at whom we boo and whistle because he incarnates not Evil but rather a one-dimensional, Western-movie stereotype of evil, starring Charles Starrett and Johnny Mack Brown:

> *. . . But the subtle Fiend,*
> *Though inly stung with anger and disdain,*
> *Dissembled, and this answer smooth returned:*
> *"Sharply thou hast insisted on rebuke,*
> *And urged me hard with doings which not will*
> *But misery hath wrested from me; where*
> *Easily canst thou find one miserable,*
> *And not enforced ofttimes to part from truth,*
> *If it may stand him more in stead to lie,*
> *Say and unsay, feign, flatter, or abjure?*
> *But thou are placed above me, thou art Lord;*
> *From thee I can and must submiss endure*
> *Check or reproof, and glad to scape so quit.*
> *Hard are the says of truth, and rough to walk,*
> *Smooth on the tongue discoursed, pleasing to th'ear,*
> *And tumble as sylvan pipe or song;*
> *What wonder then if I delight to hear*

> *Her dictates from thy mouth? Most men admire*
> *Virtue who follow not her lore. Permit me*
> *To hear thee when I come (since no man comes),*
> *And talk at least, though I despair to attain.*
> *Thy Father, who is holy, wise and pure,*
> *Suffers the hypocrite or atheous priest*
> *To tread his sacred courts, and minister*
> *About his alter, handling holy things,*
> *Praying or vowing, and vouchsafed his voice*
> *To Balaam reprobate, a prophet yet*
> *Inspired; disdain not such access to me."*
> *(Book I, 1. 465-492)*

In a psychological sense (perhaps from the stylistic standpoint too, though it is difficult to compare prose with poetry), Milton's *Paradise Regained* is immature, even infantile, when compared with Flaubert's magnificent *La Tentation de Saint Antoine*. For instance, compare the suppurating, sybaritic visions that surround Anthony, as the anchorite, in the desert of his existential despair and nausea, with Belial's attempt to convince Satan to seduce Christ with women—of all absurd things, mere women!

> *"Set women in his eye and in his walk,*
> *Among daughters of men the fairest found;*
> *Many are in each region passing fair*
> *As the noon sky, more like to goddesses*
> *Than mortal creatures, graceful and discreet,*
> *Expert in amorous arts, enchanting tongues*
> *Persuasive, virgin majesty with mild*
> *And sweet allayed, yet terrible to approach,*
> *Skilled to retire, and in retiring draw*
> *Hearts after them tangled in amorous nets.*
> *Such object hath the power to soft'n and tame*
> *Severest temper, smooth and rugged'st brow,*
> *Enerve, and with voluptuous hope dissolve,*
> *Draw out with credulous desire, and lead*
> *At will the manliest, resolutest breast,*
> *As the magnetic hardest iron draws.*
> *Women, when nothing else, beguiled the heart*
> *Of wisest Solomon, and made him build,*
> *And made him bow to the gods of his wives."*

Aware that women would be futile, Satan meets Christ on the mountain in the wilderness after his forty days' fast—and, as a titan of metaphysical Evil to the titan of conscious Good, tries to overwhelm him in his hour of greatest physical weakness. Satan tempts the Messiah with food, and Christ curtly reproves him for his adolescence. Then, again, Satan tempts him with riches, which Christ rejects with something of a cold, curling smile. He explains his position on what real wealth is, i.e., spiritual wealth, which alone matters to the immortal heart of man:

> *But to guide nations in the way of truth*
> *By saving doctrine, and from error lead*
> *To know, and knowing worship God aright,*
> *Is yet more kingly; this attracts the soul,*
> *Governs the inner man, the nobler part,*
> *That other o'er the body only reigns,*
> *And oft by force, which to a generous mind*
> *So reigning can be no sincere delight.*
> *Besides, to give a kingdom hath been thought*
> *Greater and nobler done, and to lay down*
> *Far more magnanimous, than to assume.*
> *Riches are needless then, both for themselves,*
> *And for thy reason why they should be sought,*
> *To gain a scepter, oftest better missed."*
> *(Book II, 473-86)*

In these lines, we see the principal reason for the aesthetic failure of the poem. It is Christ's moral perfection, which is nondramatic in its static quality. We realize that Milton, as a Christian, could not afford to de-emphasize the essential divinity of Christ. Yet he errs as a dramatist when he does not analyze the changes in Christ's awakening consciousness of his own divinity, at least in the physical and emotional dimensions of that religious *Erwachung*. Satan, as a protagonist, has more dimension; thus, as a character, he has a keener dramatic function. He is more of a hero, especially in the romantic sense. Of course, Satan loses a tincture of his titanism when he postures with almost masochistic obeisance before Christ, as in these totally absurd lines, which lack psychological integrity:

> *To whom the Tempter, inly racked, replied:*
> *"Let that come when it comes; all hope is lost*
> *Of my reception into grace; what worse?*
> *For where no hope is left, is left no fear.*
> *If there be worse, the expectation more*
> *Of worse torments me than the feeling can.*

> *I would be at the worst; worst is my port,*
> *My harbor and my ultimate repose,*
> *The end I would attain, my final good.*
> *My error was my error, and my crime*
> *My crime, whatever for itself condemned,*
> *And will alike be punished, whether thou*
> *Reign or reign not; though to that gentle brow*
> *Willingly I could fly, and hope thy reign,*
> *From they placid aspéct and meek regard,*
> *Rather than aggravate my evil state,*
> *Would stand between me and thy Father's ire*
> *(Whose ire I dread more than the fire of hell),*
> *A shelter and a kind of shading cool*
> *Interposition, as a summer's cloud.*
> *If I then to the worst can be haste,*
> *Why move thy feet so slow to what is best,*
> *Happiest both to thyself and all the world,*
> *That thou who are worthiest art shouldst be their king?*
>   *(Book III, 1. 203-26)*

His egotism, in short, is modified as rarely happens with the romantic hero when he fully emerges in Occidental culture in the early nineteenth century. Moreover, Milton, with "tags" that are no longer accepted by literature, concludes, typically, seemingly symptomatic of his psychological and aesthetic malaise:

> *So spake Israel's true King, and to the Fiend*
> *Made answer meet, that made void all his wiles.*
> *So fares it when with truth falsehood contends.*
>   *(Book III, 1. 441-43)*

In a sense, *Paradise Regained* is a cerebral closet drama—only that, and no more. This is its essential, undeniable character: *stasis,* as the protagonists lose themselves in the very welter of their words—indeed, their verbosity and occasional pyrotechnics. The climax, if such there is, is the verbal exchange of philosophical positions when Satan tempts Jesus in the wilderness, where, in the end, Christ summarizes his vision of truth:

> *"True image of the Father, whether throned*
> *In the bosom of bliss, and light of light*
> *Conceiving, or remote from heaven, enshrined*

In fleshly tabernacle, and human form,
Wand'ring the wilderness, whatever place,
Habit, or state, or motion, still expressing
The Son of God, with God-like force endued
Against th' attempter of thy Father's throne,
And thief of Paradise; him long of old
Thou didst debel, and down from heav'n cast
With all his army; now thou hast avenged
Supplanted Adam, and by vanquishing
Temptation hast regained lost Paradise,
And frustrated the conquest fraudulent.
He never more henceforth will dare set foot
In Paradise to tempt; his snares are broke.
For though that seat of earthly bliss be failed,
A fairer Paradise is founded now
For Adam and his chosen sons, whom thou
A Saviour art come down to reinstall;
Where they shall dwell secure, when time shall be
Of tempter and temptation without fear.
But thou, infernal Serpent, shalt not long
Rule in the clouds; like an autumnal star
Of lightning thou shalt fall from heav'n trod down
Under his feet. For proof, ere this thou feel'st
Thy wound, yet not thy last and deadliest wound,
By this repulse received, and hold'st in hell
No triumph; in all her gates Abaddon rues
Thy bold attempt. Hereafter learn with awe
To dread the Son of God: he all unarmed
Shall chase thee with the terror of his voice
From thy demoniac holds, possession foul,
Thee and thy legions; yelling they shall fly,
And beg to hide them in a herd of swine,
Lest he command them down into the deep,
Bound, and to torment sent before their time.
Hail, Son of the Most High, heir of both worlds,
Queller of Satan, on thy glorious work
Now enter, and begin to save mankind."
        (Book IV, 1. 596-635)

Yet, ironically, it is Satan who summarizes Christ's truth for Christ, for
Satan really knows the truth, a Stoic's truth laid bare, though he cannot

psychologically accommodate to it: accept it: live by it: for it: with it.

Christ, by now, has rejected the lavish banquet proffered him magically by Satan. He has also rejected the successive offers of wealth, glory, Jewish hegemony in a non-Roman Israel, and political alliances with Parthia and Rome. Succinctly, Christ states that his kingdom is not of this world—an attitude that is congruent with the Restoration emphasis on individual integrity rather than political actions. On this spiritual message, we close our consideration of *Paradise Regained* with the painful observation that it is a noble failure because neither Christ nor Satan comes off with dramatic success: they are both static, not kinetic, are not in the medieval tradition of Everyman, are not much in the heroic tradition of the Renaissance, and lack the Dionysian titanism associated with the Romantic hero of the early nineteenth century.

In our opinion, Milton's last work, *Samson Agonistes,* is also his most dramatically effective and aesthetically felicitous. Also, from the standpoint of the hero, Samson, alone with Satan, is the only satisfactory "hero" whom Milton ever delineated. And though Satan is truly a magnificent Romantic hero, worthy of Lord Byron without the wit, he is clearly not a Christian tragic hero. Our point is that Samson, though a Jew, living before the advent of Christianity, is cleary and effectively a Christian tragic hero of the first dimension in a closet drama that, to our mind, surpasses even *Paradise Lost* in depth, though of course not its breadth: scope: *envergure.*

In the drama, itself thoroughly classical, Samson is not the brawling drunkard and immature wiseacre of the Old Testament Book of *Judges.* Milton has changed him into a protagonist of sensitive conscience, integrity, piety: thus (though without the name), a Christian tragic hero, especially since Samson is Milton's idealized self, as Milton devoutly suffered through blindness and political persecution. To be sure, there are no specific Christian references in the drama, for Milton was anyway a Judeophile who in *Paradise Regained* even mocked the grandeur of a glorious pagan civilization. Yet Christian decorum, as conceived by the pietists of the Renaissance, permeates this one totally successful extended work of Milton.

It is a cerebral closet drama up to the "catastrophe" of Dagon's Temple, particularly suited to the moral sensibilities of the Christian tragic hero. In his opening speech, Samson confesses his own sinful responsibility for his pitiable lot. At the same time, in a carping way, he makes his own natural and properly egotistic complaints. Manoa, Dalila, and Harapha do give continuity and dynamic progression to the play, so that Dr. Samuel Johnson is wrong when he observes that "the play has a beginning and an end but no real middle." Gradually, through their catalytic visits, Samson's egotism and self-serving pride (itself the Greek *hamartia* of Aristotle) and even his distrust of God's eternal design surrender to selfless penitence, as his faith in God is renewed. In the end, his spirit is exalted till he becomes almost manic.

Ironically, Samson responds differently to each interlocutor from what one expects. Hence, there is a structural irony with the many niceties of Milton's exquisite ambiguities. "Agonistes," for example, is, and yet is not, something more than a contestant in a public game. Also, when blind Samson begs the slave, "A little onward lend thy guiding hand," he has truly assumed the role of the Christian tragic hero imploring a fellow penitent to pray for him, even him, and to guide him on their mutual Christian quest of Salvation.

Moreover, for once in his poetic life, Milton is not simplistic in his portraits. Manoa, the father, means well and accomplishes some good, though he is also an inept bungler. Dalila is not only treacherous and possessive, as certain critics insist; she also betrayed Samson for her own people, an act that probably any patriot would have performed for his *patrie*. Harapha is not just a simpleminded braggart but also the *bon bourgeois,* who gives a *bon bourgeois'* assessment of Samson's chastisement in the human condition. At last, transfigured by his metaphysical suffering, Samson, though blind, "sees the way"—and destroys his enemies in a bloody mass slaughter of the Philistines in Dagon's Temple.

As Professor David Daiches Raphael has pointed out in his admirable *Paradox of Tragedy,* a genuine Christian cannot suffer (or write) a tragedy because the effect is nullified by a belief in a providential God and his eternal boon of Paradise for the saved soul. But Samson is a Jew, who does not believe in the afterlife; there will be no eternal reward for him. In a word, Samson has suffered, and in the end he dies. Perhaps, enigmatically in a theological sense, and also problematically, Samson is all the more "Christian" because of the total commitment of self, psyche, and soul in the despair of a desperate existential option: suicide: the destruction of Dagon's Temple.

In his moment of truth, Samson speaks to himself, for himself, clarifying his own muddied thoughts, as he addresses his interlocutors:

> *I could be well content to try their art,*
> *Which to no few of them would prove pernicious.*
> *Yet knowing their advantages too many,*
> *Because they shall not trail me through their streets*
> *Like a wild beast, I am content to go.*

> *Masters' commands come with a power resistless*
> *To such as owe them absolute subjection;*
> *And for a life who will not change his purpose?*
> *(So mutable are all the ways of men.)*
> *Yet this be sure, in nothing to comply*
> *Scandalous or forbidden in our Law.*
> *(1. 1399-1409)*

Further, he elaborates, foreshadowing the ineluctable future, itself Calvinist:

> *Brethren, farewell; your company along*
> *I will not wish, lest it perhaps offend them*
> *To see me girt with friends; and how the sight*
> *Of me as a common enemy,*
> *So dreaded once, may now exasperate them,*
> *I know not. Lords are lordliest in their wine;*
> *And the well-feasted priest then soonest fired*
> *With zeal, if aught religion seem concerned;*
> *No less the people on their holy-days*
> *Impetuous, insolent, unquenchable;*
> *Happen what may, of me expect to hear*
> *Nothing dishonorable, impure, unworthy*
> *Our God, our Law, my nation, or myself;*
> *The last of me or no I cannot warrant.*
> *(1. 1413-26)*

After the "catastrophe" of Dagon's Temple, the chorus situates Samson within God's eternal providence—and, in its highly Greek way, also justifies the ways of God to men:

> *All is best, though we oft doubt,*
> *What the unsearchable dispose*
> *Of Highest Wisdom brings about,*
> *And ever best found in the close.*
> *Oft he seems to hide his face,*
> *But unexpectedly returns*
> *And to his faithful champion hath in place*
> *Bore witness gloriously; whence Gaza mourns,*
> *And all that band them to resist*

His uncontrollable intent:
His servants he, with new acquist
Of true experience from this great event,
With peace and consolation hath dismissed,
And calm of mind, all passion spent.
(1. 1745-58)

In the highly satisfactory protagonist of Samson, we find an Everyman on a spiritual quest, as if out of the Middle Ages; a many-faceted Renaissance hero who was a mighty warrior and witty courtier and even became something of a sage through his metaphysical suffering; and also a Romantic hero, bigger than life itself, truly titanic, capable of enormous follies and immortal deeds of high glory, as in his ultimate suicide and mass slaughter. In Milton's Christian cosmos, too, such a protagonist is ever a Christian tragic hero as he confronts a hostile, evil society that overwhelms him but simply cannot crush his indomitable spirit. Yet, ironically, Milton writes about a Jew in Samson as his most successful Christian tragic hero.

It should not concern us that in *Samson Agonistes* Milton does not even allude to Christianity, since, indeed, he never waxed properly theological even in *Paradise Lost* and *Paradise Regained*. On the whole, Milton's theology, if such it may be called, is as blandly innocuous as his protagonists' paper-thin psychology. Enigmatically, too, for this great poet (great, yes, despite himself), who so lamentably deprecated pagan thought and art in *Paradise Regained,* penned the most perfect Greek tragedy in English literature on a Hebrew subject as a Christian tragic hero! Where but in the late Renaissance could we find the full flowering of such disparate genius, and with Milton at that as the greatest technical master of English along with James Joyce, and on a Jewish subject explicitly devoid of Christian themes as an incomparable implicit portrait of the Christian tragic hero?

Here, with the hero, is found at once Milton's incredible strength and also his insufferable weakness. Let us take an analogy from the cinéma, which interests us all in our visually oriented society. Let us compare Milton with Dante, who came before him and whose *Divine Comedy* is a kind of *La Dolce Vita,* that great Federico Fellini film about contemporary Roman decadence: a picture of individual souls on fire, so spiritually intense that the Catholic Church gave it a special, approved rating. Or let us compare Milton with Baudelaire, whose *Fleurs du mal* is our contemporary *Divine Comedy* in its aesthetics of evil, and whose attenuated sensuality reminds us of *Blood and Roses,* that ignored masterpiece, as it arouses our passions in its sheer decadence. But Milton's epics, *Paradise Lost, Paradise Regained,* and

Samson Agonistes, are like those technically magnificent silent films of the incomparable D.W. Griffith; for example, *The Birth of a Nation* and *Babylon,* which, despite the exaggerated gestures and paper-thin grandiloquence of the protagonists, move us with a certain almost surrealist sense of the sublime at the same time they make us smile to ourselves with a kind of bittersweetness over our irrevocable loss of a far simpler world, now vanished, which will never again exist in time and space.

William Blake as Christian Tragic Hero

Without question, Edmund Spenser, William Blake, and William Butler Yeats, more than any other English writers, have attracted a considerable body of what the existentialists might properly call "absurdité." In truth, certain ingenious critics have devoted themselves to admirable but highly impressionistic exegeses of the allegorical writings of Spenser and Yeats and of what we prefer to call the apocalyptic writings of William Blake. We refer specifically to David Erdman in *Blake, Prophet against Empire,* who prefers (rather one-dimensionally, we fear) political allegories in the apocalyptic writings, which really are rooted in the Books of *Daniel* and *Revelation.* Northrop Frye, in *Fearful Symmetry,* probably because he is an intellectual historian, sees metaphysical dimensions in what we still maintain is essentially apocalyptic literature, much of it also in the lineage of the Biblical *Apocrypha.* Indeed, these men wax more poetic than Blake himself in their sophisticated subtleties as headily cerebral examinations of what Blake simplistically never intended. On a more modest and far saner note are Mona Wilson's *The Life of William Blake* and Robert F. Gleckner's *The Piper and the Bard.* More perceptive, still, is Arthur Symons' *William Blake,* which modern critics fail to appreciate for its direct empathies, though they do acknowledge the splendor of Swinburne's essay and the cogency of T. S. Eliot's.

Of this, we are heartily sorry because one day Symons may be accorded the title he so nobly deserves as one of the three great English critics, along with Dr. Samuel Johnson and Matthew Arnold. While generous, Symons saw Blake's very real limitations as well as his unique contributions, a stance that recent Blake enthusiasts decry. We explicitly state what Symons seems to imply: that Blake is strong only when he impressionistically writes the most symbolic lyrics, and that the rest of the time he lamentably fails, since his poetic execution cannot equal his mystical *envergure,* and this causes in readers a tension that they cannot dismiss or even reconcile. For Blake, above all, was a Christian mystic, a kind of delightfully eccentric and visionary (and maybe also psychotic) heretic to Swedenborg's own heresy. Still, Blake is a Christian tragic hero, though he doesn't realize this dimension of himself, preferring to think of himself as "the last happy man." And it is as the Christian tragic hero that we shall now consider him from the lyrics of his two great early collections, *Songs of Innocence* and *Songs of Experience.* The apocalyptic writings, we feel, are only noble failures that never truly communicate the poet's mystical visions to us, since Blake's mythology is so individual, particular, peculiar, personal that it doesn't really fit into the Judeo-Christian world view.

Essentially, all contemporary critics on Blake have erred because they though he was a schematic writer. This point of view is manifestly absurd. Was any mystic, as Blake was, ever schematic; or did Blake, rather, merely write down in aphorisms his disconnected glimpses into the infinite? Blake was no allegorist, either, as only the naive can believe. Instead, he was a symbolist in a very fragmented way, so that his long works are not truly epics but rather mosaics—or, perhaps, *pointilliste* paintings. The tragedy is that Blake, who thought he was the reincarnation of Milton, conceived of himself as an epic writer for modern man. The key to understanding Blake is the symbol or, even more narrowly, the image, for Blake foreshadowed symbolism and imagism. It is through the symbol and image of noteworthy individual poems that we now purpose to study Blake.

The well-known citation from "Auguries of Innocence" admirably denotes what Blake is really about in his Spinozian God-intoxication:

> *To see a World in a Grain of Sand*
> *And a Heaven in a Wild Flower*
> *Hold infinity in the palm of your hand*
> *And Eternity in an hour.*

In other words, whatever he may or may not be in his probably schizophrenic Swedenborgianism, Blake is also a pantheist. In this light, among the Romantics, Blake, even more than William Wordsworth, apocalyptically foresaw the horrows of the Industrial Revolution and the ensuing age of technocracy with its basic antihumanism and political Caesarism. For Wordsborth, then, nature was ever good, and certainly Blake subscribed to the romantic cult of the Noble Savage. Yet this rather trite observation is not always true. Toward his hometown of London, as a cockney out of his element in the verdant countryside he professed to love, Blake evidences an ambivalent attitude, as in these memorable lines from "London":

I wander thro' each charter'd street,
Near where the charter'd Thames does flow.
And mark in every face I meet
Masks of weakness, masks of woe.

In every cry of every Man,
In every Infants cry of fear,
In every voice: in every ban.
The mind-forg'd manacles I hear

Now the Chimney-sweepers cry
Every blackning Church appalls.
And the hapless Soldiers sigh
Runs in blood down Palace walls

But most thro' midnight streets I hear
How the youthful Harlots curse
Blasts the new born Infants tear
And blights with plagues the Marriage hearse.
(From Songs of Experience)

We impressionistically characterized this poem "ambivalent" by design. The mock horror at the crassness of cruel London shows a certain almost sadomasochistic apprehension and appreciation of the metaphysical evil of urban life in the early days of the Industrial Revolution. The image is double: and fused. Intellectually, Blake expresses horror (truly a Christian horror) at this life, decadent, though not out of *la dolce vita.* Emotionally, however, it draws him irresistibly on: sucks him into the very vortex of existential thinginess in his despair and nausea, so to speak: because Blake mystically identifies with London and incorporates the city into his psyche, soul, self. For Blake is not only nature but also artificial London, and his being includes these antipodes in the totality of his horrified poetic experience as a Christian mystic. To posture for nature is not necessarily to take a stance against London (dehumanized technocracy), since London, enigmatically, also problematically, is also part of nature. As a mystic, Blakes includes opposites in his philosophical system, if such it may be called, just as the Eastern mystics did, in contradistinction to Aristotle's *either . . . or* dichotomies, corollaries, and postulates.

"Posture," yes, for we can use that word applicably in regard to Blake. Was he always the "happy fool," as literary historians have so quaintly and perhaps so absurdly observed of him? Was Blake's perpetual exaltation not the infallible sign of his mania—or, as the psychiatrists would say, his depression—as the other side of the psychological coin? Perhaps it was. Certainly, we posit that it may have been—and that, psychologically, it must have been. Did not all of the great mystics have their crises, their moments of doubt, before they achieved their religious moments of enlightenment? Manifestly so, as we know from all hagiography, without exception.

Are we, then, to believe that Blake alone was always so manic, so "high," in his religious exaltation that he didn't secretly lust for harlots and thirst for the gold fineries of damnation and filthy lucre? Impressionistically, we feel, conjecture, and intuit that Blake, psychologically, empathized with the great doubters—Newton, Voltaire, Rousseau—whom he pretended to decry in horror at his own open-mouthed, even salivating admiration. Too, destitute as he was during his entire life, did he not, like all of us, yearn for the creature comforts that money, as Balzac pointed out, can always buy for us in the technocracy of modern civilization? With our minds, most of all in our critical guts, we intuit that we must not take Blake at face value whenever he professes total faith, certitude, conviction all the time. For all other mystics, including Buddha himself, wavered, had reservations, doubts, metaphysical hesitations, which obviated their existential options for Faith: i.e., the immediate and total apprehension of God, imagistically conceived and metaphorically executed, as in the best poems of Blake in his two early volumes, where he presents himself as the Christian tragic hero.

Do the psychiatric sophisticates among our readers get the philosophical point? There is in contemporary psychiatry a school of communications theory called double-bind depth therapy, first developed by the Bateson group at Palo Alto, and popularized by Mme Sèchehaye of Paris, Dr. Jakob Rosen of New York City, and Dr. Carl A. Whitaker of Atlanta. The point in double-bind depth therapy is that, indeed, all communication is double by its very nature. One cannot simply say "I love you" or "I hate you." Instead, if one is truthful, one is always saying "I love hate you," even when one verbalizes "I love you" or "I hate you." The psychotic is sick, then, precisely because he cannot decode the message sent by his partner, originally his schizophrenogenic mother; in this light, we wish we had details about Blake's relationship to his mother, though we already know what we would surely find.

In the case of maladjustment, the psychotic transcribes literally but not emotionally the message "I love you" from the schizophrenogenic mother, though she really means "I hate your goddamn guts, baby boy." In this guise, we feel that Blake was not a true mystic, and certainly not an orthodox Christian mystic, but rather a schizophrenic, since in double-bind depth therapy the manic-depressive psychosis is merely a desperate defense against the disassociation and fragmentation and compartmentalization of classical schizophrenia: a psychological evasion through manic "highs" and depressive "lows," and in Blake's case a flight (too) through poetic fantasy, itself a release of the organizing forces of the chaotic unconscious.

For the unconscious mind is nothing if not creativity, i.e., the poetic process, of which Blake (though admittedly not a major poet, even within the English romantic movement) is a prime example. This creativity depends upon what the Greeks would call harmony—and upon what the modern psychologists would call the harnessing of affect; certainly, despite his obvious poetic, philosophical, and religious limitations, nobody could surpass Blake in this singular respect. Poetic inspiration, or (as in this case) the romantic inspiration, is the kinetic outflow of what Henri Bergson would later call the *élan vital,* or motor force of man in the human condition. When successful, this *process* results in the properly *static* effect of accomplished and finished art: yes, in *stasis,* since great literature is the crystallization of our immortal moment of eternal time. Now, to be sure, Blake does not often achieve the level of great art, since he rarely crystallizes such immortal moments of eternal time in works of *stasis* that represent *kinesis*. But he demonstrably does at times. And when he does, it is always in the light and the singular purlieu of the Christian tragic hero.

Blake consciously thought that childhood represented innocence—in our case, the lost innocence of the natural life, though no psychiatrist would be so naïve as to believe that. For the psychological sophisticate, childhood, indeed, represents the chaos of the pure id, a fact Blake seems to have repressed, as he tries so demonstrably to put his picture of the Christian tragic hero before us this time, in the radiant and even beatific form of the "Innocent Child." For example, these lines of "Infant Joy" read most instructively:

> *I have no name*
> *I am but two days old,—*
> *What shall I call thee?*
> *I happy am*
> *Joy is my name,—*
> *Sweet joy befall thee!*
>
> *Pretty joy!*
> *Sweet joy but two days old,*
> *Sweet joy I call thee;*
> *Thou dost smile.*

> *I sing the while*
> *Sweet joy befall thee.*
>   *(From Songs of Innocence)*

In "The Little Vagabond," the "innocent child" assumes the role of the street gypsy (the *gamin*, as if Gavroche from Victor Hugo's *Les Misérables)*, who, though he has seen raw street life, still retains his stance of innocence:

> *Dear Mother, dear Mother, the Church is cold.*
> *But the Ale-house is healthy & pleasant & warm;*
> *Besides I can tell where I am use'd well,*
> *Such usage in heaven will never do well.*
>
> *But if at the Church they would give us some Ale.*
> *And a pleasant fire, our souls to regale;*
> *We'd sing and we'd pray, all the live-long day:*
> *Nor ever once wish from the Church to stray.*
>
> *Then the Parson might preach & drink & sing.*
> *And we'd be as happy as birds in the spring:*
> *And modest dame Lurch, who is always at Church,*
> *Would not have bandy children nor fasting nor birch.*
>
> *And God like a father rejoicing to see,*
> *His children as pleasant and happy as he:*
> *Would have no more quarrel with the Devil or the Barrel*
> *But kiss him & give him both drink and apparel.*
>   *(From Songs of Experience)*

It is in such a poem that Blake's persona of the "innocent child," absorbed in God's grace, cracks, splinters, and fragments. God, really, doesn't come off so well in this poem, as the Devil, surely a more humane and compassionate figure, just as the tavernkeepers participate in humanity more than the Christian does in the Satanist crucible of London. Moreover, almost startlingly, Blake does not establish good and evil as antipodes, but he rather subsumes evil in good. In a sense, therefore, there is no evil, just as in this peculiar particularity the carnality of creature comforts comes off far better than orthodox Christianity.

In a sense, Blake pursues this leitmotif, a constant concern in his work, in the "Garden of Love":

I went to the Garden of Love.
And saw what I never had seen:
A Chapel was built in the midst.
Where I used to play on the green.

And the gates of this Chapel were shut,
And Thou shalt not, writ over the door;
So I turn'd to the Garden of Love,
That so many sweet flowers bore,

And I saw it was filled with graves.
And tomb-stones where flowers should be:
And Priests in black gowns, were walking their rounds,
And binding with briars my joys & desires.
    (From Songs of Experience)

Once again, Blake, clearly, emphatically, does not posture (in what existentialists call "absurdity") with a kind of one-dimensional orthodox Christianity. Moreover, he emphasizes and reinforces this position in "The School Boy":

I love to rise in a summer morn,
When the birds sing on every tree;
The distant huntsman winds his horn,
And the sky-lark sings with me.
O! what sweet company.

But to go to school in a summer morn
O! it drives all joy away;
Under a cruel eye outworn,
The little ones spend the day,
In sighing and dismay.

Ah! then at times I drooping sit,
And spend many an anxious hour.
Nor in my book can I take delight,
Nor sit in learnings bower,
Worn thro' with the dreary shower.

How can the bird that is born for joy,
Sit in a cage and sing.

> *How can a child when fears annoy,*
> *But droop his tender wing.*
> *And forget his youthful spring.*
>
> *O! father and mother, if buds are nip'd,*
> *And blossoms blown away,*
> *And if the tender plants are strip'd*
> *Of their joy in the springing day.*
> *By sorrow and cares dismay.*
>
> *How shall the summer arise in joy.*
> *Or the summer fruits appear.*
> *Or how shall we gather what griefs destroy*
> *Or bless the mellowing year.*
> *When the blasts of winter appear.*
>   *(From Songs of Experience)*

Surely, from a consideration of these lines, only a naïve reader would consider Blake to be the archetypal poet of "lost innocence," for his Christian tragic hero never loses that sense of "lost innocence" but rather carries it ever with him, and it was never much of an innocence anyway in the Biblical sense of Adam and Eve in the Garden of Eden. To be sure, Blake is not always successful in his poetic efforts. But he is subtle, though not sophisticated, and always quite ironic. Thereby, he sometimes achieves remarkable effects, particularly in painting portraits of the Christian tragic hero.

To redirect our inquiry somewhat, what is God but love: divine love? Certainly, this is the ultimate meaning of the Christian message in Blake for his exemplary poem "The Divine Image":

> *To Mercy Pity Peace and Love,*
> *All pray in their distress:*
> *And to these virtues of delight*
> *Return their thankfulness.*
>
> *For Mercy Pity Peace and Love,*
> *Is God our father dear:*
> *And Mercy Pity Peace and Love.*
> *Is Man his child and care.*
>
> *For Mercy has a human heart*
> *Pity, a human face:*

And Love, the human form divine,
And Peace, the human dress.

Then every man of every clime,
That prays in his distress,
Prays to the human form divine
Love Mercy Pity Peace.

And all must love the human form,
In heathen, turk or jew.
Where Mercy Love & Pity dwell
There God is dwelling too.
        (From Songs of Innocence)

So, where Love dwells (along with Mercy and Pity, surely great Christian virtues), there dwells the essence of God. Certainly, as Catholic critics, we would agree to that somewhat trite observation about man in the human condition. But why do we maintain, unlike most critics, that Blake was not always happy transfigured in his mysticism, but rather only *desperately* happy in the very Christian sense of deep *despair.* For just as in the masks of drama we have both the smiling mask and the weeping mask, so, too, in the singular William Blake we see both exaltation and despair, not exaltation in despair (either), but, rather, exaltation because of that existential despair: in the *engagement,* or existential option for love that the Christian tragic hero forces himself to make in spite of the abulia that paralyzes his free will in the chamber of metaphysical horrors of Blake's Industrial Revolution, so soon to sweep the entire world in the age of technocracy.

Against such a drab, ugly, crass world, Blake sets the "natural world" depicted beautiful by "Laughing Song":

When the green woods laugh with the voice of joy
And the dimpling stream runs laughing by,
When the air does laugh with our merry wit,
And the green hill laughs with the noise of it.

When the meadows laugh with lively green
And the grasshopper laughs in the merry scene,
When Mary and Susan and Emily.
With their sweet round mouths sing Ha, Ha, He.

When the painted birds laugh in the shade
Where our table with cherries and nuts is spread

> *Come live & be merry and join with me,*
> *To sing the sweet chorus of Ha, Ha, He.*
>   *(From Songs of Innocence)*

The further one departs from "natural goodness" and degenerates into "organized religion," itself symptomatic of the curse of civilization, the more one participates in, or is beguiled by, the metaphysical dimensions of pure evil, even when it is cloaked under religion, as in this self-explanatory poem, "Holy Thursday":

> *Twas on a Holy Thursday their innocent faces clean*
> *The children walking two & two in red & blue & green*
> *Grey headed beadles walked before with wands as white as snow*
> *Till into the high dome of Pauls they like Thames waters flow*
>
> *O what a multitude they seemed these flowers of London town*
> *Seated in companies they sit with radiance all their own*
> *The hum of multitudes was there but multitudes of lambs*
> *Thousands of little boys & girls raising their innocent hands*
>
> *Now like a mighty wind they raise to heaven the voice of song*
> *Or like harmonious thunderings the seats of heaven among*
> *Beneath them sit the aged men wise guardians of the poor*
> *Then cherish pity, lest you drive an angel from your door*
>   *(From Songs of Innocence)*

The verses are singularly moving, and the last line reaches a deeply moving climax with an acerbic comment upon "Nature's child" in the bosom of the Established Church of England, which never understood Blake, just as, in truth, Blake never understood it, either.

There are three series of poems that portray "Nature's innocent (guileless?) Child" against the background of London—and, by extension, the dehumanizing age of technocracy. One series is on the "Chimney Sweeper," as in these lines from the poems by that name:

> *When my mother died I was very young*
> *And my father sold me while yet my tongue,*
> *Could scarcely cry weep weep weep weep.*
> *So your chimneys I sweep & in soot I sleep.*
>
> *Theres little Tom Dacre, who cried when his head*
> *That curl'd like a lambs back, was shav'd, so I said.*

Hush Tom never mind it, for when your head's bare,
You know that the soot cannot spoil your white hair.

And so he was quiet, & that very night.
As Tom was a sleeping he had such a sight,
That thousands of sweepers Dick, Joe Net & Jack
Were all of them lock'd up in coffins of black

And by came an Angel who had a bright key
And he open'd the coffins & set them all free,
Then down a green plain leaping laughing they run
And wash in a river and shine in the Sun.

Then naked & white, all their bags left behind,
They rise upon clouds, and sport in the wind.
And the Angel told Tom if he'd be a good boy,
He'd have God for his father & never want joy.

And so Tom awoke and we rose in the dark
And got with our bags & our brushes to work.
Tho' the morning was cold, Tom was happy & warm,
So if all do their duty, they need not fear harm.
     (From Songs of Innocence)

A little black thing among the snow:
Crying weep, weep. in notes of woe!
Where are thy father & mother? say?
They are both gone up to the church to pray.

Because I was happy upon the heath.
And smil'd among the winters snow:
They clothed me in the clothes of death.
And taught me to sing the notes of woe.

And because I am happy. & dance & sing.
They think they have done me no injury:
And are gone to praise God & his Priest & King
Who make up a heaven of our misery.
     (From Songs of Experience)

The tension between nature (ideality) and the technological age (reality: drab, crass, cold, cruel) is almost unbearable in the very sophisticated and ever subtle verses of Blake. Here, as a Christian tragic hero, he is truly a voice crying from the wilderness, or, as Eliot later called it aptly enough, the Wasteland.

In the second series of "Nature's child," suffering behind the smile in the painted veil of the human condition, we see "The Little Boy Lost" and "The Little Boy Found":

> *Father, father, where are you going*
> *O do not walk so fast.*
> *Speak father, speak to your little boy*
> *Or else I shall be lost,*
>
> *The night was dark no father was there*
> *The child was wet with dew.*
> *The mire was deep. & the child did weep*
> *And away the vapour flew.*
> *(From Songs of Innocence)*
>
> *The little boy was lost in the lonely fen,*
> *Led by the wand'ring light.*
> *Began to cry, but God ever nigh,*
> *Appeard like his father in white.*
>
> *He kissed the child & by the hand led*
> *And to his mother brought.*
> *Who in sorrow pale, thro' the lonely dale*
> *Her little boy weeping sought.*
> *(From Songs of Innocence)*

To our mind, in a race-conscious America of the late twentieth century, one of the most moving poems Blake ever wrote is "The Little Black Boy":

> *My mother bore me in the southern wild,*
> *And I am black, but O! my soul is white;*
> *White as an angel is the English child:*
> *But I am black as if bereav'd of light.*
>
> *My mother taught me underneath a tree*
> *And sitting down before the heat of day,*
> *She took me on her lap and kissed me.*
> *And pointing to the east began to say.*

Look on the rising sun: there God does live
And gives his light, and gives his heat away.
And flowers and trees and beasts and men recieve (sic)
Comfort in morning joy in the noon day.

And we are put on earth a little space,
That we may learn to bear the beams of love,
And these black bodies and this sun-burnt face
Is but a cloud, and like a shady grove.

For when our souls have learn'd the heat to bear
The cloud will vanish we shall hear his voice.
Saying: come out from the grove my love & care,
And round my golden tent like lambs rejoice.

Thus did my mother say and kissed me,
And thus I say to little English boy.
When I from black and he from white cloud free.
And round the tent of God like lambs we joy:

Ill shade him from the heat till he can bear
To lean in joy upon our fathers knee.
And then I'll stand and stroke his silver hair,
And be like him and he will then love me.
        (From Songs of Innocence)

But in his veritable cult of attenuated *lingam-yoni,* Blake is also concerned with the female principle, not so much as the antipode as the metaphysical complement to the male principle. We see this quite clearly in our quatrains from the rather long poem (a long lyric for Blake, that is), "The Little Girl Lost":

In futurity
I prophetic see.
That the earth from sleep
(Grave the sentence deep)

Shall arise and seek
For her maker meek:
And the desart wild
Become a garden mild.

In the southern clime,
Where the summers prime,
Never fades away;
Lovely Lyca lay.

Seven summers old
Lovely Lyca told,
She had wanderd long,
Hearing wild birds song.

Sweet sleep come to me
Underneath this tree;
Do father, mother weep.—
"Where can Lyca sleep".

Lost in desert wild
Is your little child.
How can Lyca sleep,
If her mother weep.

If her heart does ake,
Then let Lyca wake;
If my mother sleep,
Lyca shall not weep.

Frowning frowning night,
O'er this desert bright.
Let thy moon arise.
While I close my eyes.

Sleeping Lyca lay;
While the beasts of prey,
Come from caverns deep,
View'd the maid asleep

The kingly lion stood
And the virgin view'd,
Then he gambold round
O'er the hallowd ground:

Leopards, tygers play,

Round her as she lay;
While the lion old,
Bow'd his mane of gold.

And her bosom lick,
And upon her neck,
From his eyes of flame,
Ruby tears there came;

While the lioness
Loos'd her slender dress,
And naked they convey'd
To caves the sleeping maid.
        (From Songs of Experience)

But Blake is concerned with dynamic progression, i.e., kinesis, spiritual movement, and so relocates the female principle in time and space in "The Little Girl Found":

All the night in woe,
Lyca's parents go:
Over vallies deep.
While the desarts weep.

Tired and woe-begone.
Hoarse with making moan:
Arm in arm seven days.
They trac'd the desert ways.

Seven nights they sleep.
Among shadows deep:
And dream they see their child
Starv'd in desert wild.

Pale thro' pathless ways
The fancied image strays.
Famish'd, weeping, weak
With hollow piteous shriek

Rising from unrest,
The trembling woman prest,

With feet of weary woe;
She could no further go.

In his arms he bore.
Her arm'd with sorrow sore;
Till before their way,
A couching lion lay.

Turning back was vain,
Soon his heavy mane.
Bore them to the ground;
Then he stalk'd around.

Smelling to his prey.
But their fears allay.
When he licks their hands;
And silent by them stands.

They look upon his eyes
Fill'd with deep surprise:
And wondering behold,
A spirit arm'd in gold.

On his head a crown
On his shoulders down.
Flow'd his golden hair.
Gone was all their care.

Follow me he said,
Weep not for the maid;
In my palace deep,
Lyca lies asleep.

Then they followed.
Where the vision led:
And saw their sleeping child,
Among tygers wild.

To this day they swell
In a lonely dell

Nor fear the wolvish howl,
Nor the lions growl.
(From Songs of Experience)

Consequently, the aspects of woman are also aspects of man, for in the metaphysical sense both are subsumed in the hermaphroditism of totality of being, as, indeed, the men and women of Blake's engravings all appear peculiarly hermaphroditic, i.e., sexless, at the same time that they are truly sensual as androgynes.

Blake is also interested in animals, especially as they symbolize man: or, perhaps, types of men. In this light, one of his most famous and often quoted poems is "The Lamb":

> *Little Lamb who made thee*
> *Dost thou know who made thee*
> *Gave thee life & bid thee feed.*
> *By the stream & o'er the mead;*
> *Gave thee clothing of delight,*
> *Softest clothing wooly bright;*
> *Gave thee such a tender voice,*
> *Making all the vales rejoice:*
> *Little Lamb who made thee*
> *Dost thou know who made thee*
>
> *Little Lamb I'll tell thee,*
> *Little Lamb I'll tell thee;*
> *He is called by thy name,*
> *For he calls himself a Lamb:*
> *He is meek & he is mild,*
> *He became a little child:*
> *I a child & thou a lamb,*
> *We are called by his name.*
> *Little Lamb God bless thee.*
> *Little Lamb God bless thee.*
> *(From Songs of Innocence)*

Of course, the "lamb" is literally a lamb, but also spiritually Christ, and also spiritually man in the worship of Christ in the brotherhood of man under the rule of love.

Perhaps Blake's most dramatically successful poem is "The Tyger":

Tyger Tyger, burning bright,
In the forest of the night;
What immortal hand or eye,
Could frame thy fearful symmetry?

In what distant deeps or skies.
Burnt the fire of thine eyes?
On what wings dare he aspire?
What the hand, dare sieze (sic) the fire?

And what shoulder, & what art,
Could twist the sinews of thy heart?
And when thy heart began to beat,
What dread hand? & what dread feet?

What the hammer? what the chain,
In what furnace was thy brain?
What the anvil? what dread grasp,
Dare its deady terrors clasp?

When the stars threw down their spears
And water'd heaven with their tears:
Did he smile his work to see?
Did he who made the Lamb make thee?

Tyger Tyger burning bright,
In the forests of the night:
What immortal hand or eye,
Dare frame thy fearful symmetry?
    (From Songs of Experience)

Just as the "Lamb" was Christ, or Nature, or Goodness, or Process in Man, so, too, "The Tyger" is certainly Nature (in its Dionysian and not Apollonian character) and perhaps also is God. Certainly, whatever its ultimate dimensions of meaning are, it is aesthetically a pleasing and powerful poem.

All of these images are aspects of the Christian tragic hero. Nowhere is his posture before good and evil, God and Satan, ideality and reality, nature and technocracy, more apparent than in "A Poison Tree":

I was angry with my friend;
I told my wrath, my wrath did end.
I was angry with my foe;
I told it not, my wrath did grow.

And I waterd it in fears,
Night & morning with my tears:
And I sunned it with smiles,
And with soft deceitful wiles.

And it grew both day and night,
Till it bore an apple bright.
And my foe beheld it shine,
And he knew that it was mine.

And into my garden stole.
When the night had veild the pole;
In the morning glad I see;
My foe outstretchd beneath the tree.
   (From Songs of Experience)

In this admirable poem, Blake seems to posit, almost existentially, that man creates good or evil through his options, defined in the social and cosmic context of those options, and that without intent those existential options lose their metaphysical connection with good and evil—and are thus only tags, empty appellations, no more than that, if indeed that much. Would not this insight into the Christian tragic hero in the despair of choice please all contemporary Christian existentialists, since they believe and profess very much the same thing?

In retrospect, as we stated at the outset, we have restricted ourselves to a consideration of the Christian tragic hero in the lyrics rather than in the apocalyptic writing, which Erdman erroneously calls political allegories, and which Frye erroneously considers metaphysical poems. Regretfully, we feel that this apocalyptic literature was all too ambitious for Blake's technical gifts, which were very small and more than a little shrill. In truth, we agree wholeheartedly with traditional criticism that Blake is the thinnest and shrillest voice of the English Romantic poets. We do not at all see in him the major English writer Professor Erdman professes to see. Clearly, Blake's gifts were quite limited; and his Christian heresies, which are enormous in his private mythology, make it difficult for him to communicate verbally and pictorially within the guiding and established framework of the Judeo-Christian world view. We believe that Blake wrote only a dozen or so power-ful lyrics, of which three or four will be justly anthologized as long as English poetry survives: primarily, too, survive for their imagistic aspects in the Christian tragic hero. But to see in Blake more than that is to be off center, truly eccentric, from the mainstream of English historical criticism.

Indeed, two writers come to mind whenever we think of Blake. First, he has certain parallels to Gérard de Nerval, a French Christian mystic of the nineteenth century, whose hallucinatory writing resembles Blake's in the particularities of their mutual schizophrenia, for both were painfully psy-chotic as well as visionary. But Nerval is a more skillful poet and a far more polished prose writer. Too, in his vast apocalyptic literature, Blake approx-imates in poetry what our own James Branch Cabell does in prose with his mythical kingdom of Poictesme. Cabell had his vogue, which is now long past except for *Jurgen* and *The Silver Stallion,* just as Blake is currently enjoying an unmerited vogue, which will surely also pass. For like Nerval and Cabell, Blake is merely an enchanted flutist, though one of genius, limited genius, in the fabulously rich orchestra of nineteenth-century and modern Romantic literature.

T. S. Eliot as
Christian Tragic Hero

Despite a plethora of literary allusions and a seeming fragmentation or compartmentalization, there is an astonishing unity in the poems and plays of T. S. Eliot. Perhaps this unity—almost surrealistic at times, and always highly impressionistic—assumes two dimensions. First, there is a "Christian community"—or, as the Church Fathers called it during the very birth of Christianity, *koinonia:* a kind of Christian communist community. Second, there is a central concern with love: the Greek *agape* of the early Church, and the (Latin) *caritas* of the High Middle Ages, when Catholicism was at its pinnacle with Dante Alighieri, as Eliot's own poet of preference.

Moreover, these two themes are interrelated. For Eliot, who seems asexual despite certain scabrous phrases, ever perceives Christian love (*agape, caritas*) as the very cement that holds the Christian communist community (*koinonia*) intact: together. Within the world (this "present evil aeon," as the Church Fathers called it), the Christian, by definition, is something of a tragic hero. This is especially true of Eliot himself as a poet of existential despair, nausea, abulia, neurasthenia, even madness within the admittedly anti-Christian madness of the modern world, degenerating into the insanities of Communism, National Socialism, Falangism, and (as Eliot might add with a merry wink) into democracy itself.

At the same time, there is a strong Stoic element in Eliot, of which he seems somewhat unaware, with his Christian bias against even the noblest of all pagan philosophies. By this, we refer to the Stoic love of, preoccupation with, even obsession with truth laid bare, just as Oedipus obsessively pursued truth to the point of his own destruction. We do not feel that truth, so conceived, really plays this overwhelming role in a Christian religion preoccupied with (and perhaps obsessed with) service and fraternity within the pagan brotherhood of man, itself also originally a Stoic doctrine.

What, then, is truth for Eliot as a Christian tragic hero? It is reality. Man must see reality, and he must see it (and thereby understand it) as a whole. Consequently, Eliot, in his criticism, is drawn to those poets like Dante and Shakespeare who envision the totality of human experience, while he voices lesser encomia for Goethe and Milton, who do not encompass the whole of the *catholicity* of man—or, as for Eliot, Christian man, ever acting in a rational and well-ordered Christian cosmos.

In his academic training, we must remember that Eliot was a formal philosopher; he was a man of letters mostly through self-instruction, which he carried out with brilliance. As a philosopher, therefore, he was concerned most especially (as in his perceptive dissertation on F. H. Bradley) with reality—or, more properly, how we apprehend reality. In this light, it was Immanuel Kant who first formulated that we can never know *das Ding-an-sich* (the thing-in-itself) but rather only know our sense impressions of it. Though Kant was the greatest of the German idealists, the logical positivists in the lineage of their founder, Auguste Comte, would surely agree: Emphatically. Eliot, in a way, seems to entertain this solipsism; for this reason, he is an *impressionist,* as a man of letters, in the etymological sense of "impressionism."

At this point, however, Eliot radically departs from the German idealism of Kant (himself a skeptic), and, most emphatically, from the logical positivists. After all, for them, truth is merely statistics: what happens, and properly not why it happens, which, most regrettably, is always speculative in nature. In other words, since the sun has always risen in the east and set in the west, the logical positivist assumes that this will always be true; but he hastens to add that he knows only what has happened (statistically, too) and can never *ultimately* understand why it happened. Thus, as we all know, the logical positivists, who dominate modern philosophy, even dictatorially, are the mathematicians and scientists.

Eliot, nevertheless, is an Anglo-Catholic, who subscribes to the poetic vision of Dante and to the dogmas of Saint Thomas Aquinas in the medieval formulations of Catholicism. They hold that truth, rather, is a matter of *coherence:* that it fits together like pieces of a jigsaw puzzle, so that man can at last glimpse the big picture, or, rather, as they think of it, the eternal design of God, in itself ultimate reality, especially in its spiritual dimensions. Thus, properly, they are philosophical *essentialists,* who hold that *essence* (or design) precedes *existence* (or being).

Eliot is in this tradition, an essentialist who emphatically subscribes to the coherence theory of truth. He uses impressions, glimpsed and governed solipsistically, to be sure; but they add up and make sense for him, since he is a Catholic who believes in coherence: in the ultimate apprehension of eternal design, or God. If this is true of Eliot (and it demonstrably is), then why should he be a Christian tragic hero at all? Indeed, how can any Christian really be a tragic hero? For no matter what happens to him in this vale of tears, he is assured of ultimate salvation, Paradise, if only he dies in a state of grace. This, ultimately, is the message of Christianity. In his Anglo-Catholic orthodoxy (and what is Anglo-Catholicism, originally, but the English Catholicism of the High Middle Ages?), Eliot demonstrably subscribes to Christianity. Yet, problematically—even enigmatically, too—he posits himself as his own Christian tragic hero.

Or does he? In comparison, Baudelaire is always his own poet-hero (and thus his own Christian tragic hero), but this is not really true of Eliot. For in his poems and plays, he presents a long and often surprisingly disparate *dramatis personae,* who are just that, *personae*—not just masks, but theatrical persons who wear masks only sometimes, frequently to dupe others (to be sure) even more than to deceive themselves in their existential despair and nausea. Collectively, all of these characters may very well be Eliot, as his own Christian tragic hero. Individually, however, they represent only certain facets of Eliot (always changing, shifting, metamorphosing diurnally, for Eliot subscribes to Heracleitus' notion that life is *kinesis,* or constant change). Hence, they are the individual Christian heroes with whom we shall first concern ourselves in a kind of cursory analysis. Then we shall postulate our own synthesis of them in Eliot himself as the Christian tragic hero who permeates his poems and plays—and who, indeed, is reflected, though obliquely, in his criticism, which is not our concern here.

At this point, while analyzing themes and *personae,* we intend to foreshadow our aesthetic evaluation of Eliot—and to outrage contemporary criticism—by claiming that Eliot is at his strongest in the early poems and the tragic plays, while he is at his weakest in "The Waste Land," "The Four Quartets," and his comic plays. All the reasons why we make this startling assessment will become clear later. Suffice it, for the moment, to state that Eliot needs a strong tragic hero, though often only implicitly Christian, to hang his impressions on and around, as he does so admirably in the early poems and the tragedies, and as he fails to do (in the noblest failures ever written) in "The Waste Land," "The Four Quartets," and the comedies. In a word, Eliot ever succeeds laudably when he zeros in on a specific Christian tragic hero as a salient facet of himself; and he ever fails when he waxes diffuse without a central Christian tragic hero, as in "The Waste Land," "The Four Quartets," and the comedies.

Impressionism, yes, and above all, solipsism, since that is the philosophical term for literary impressionism: Especially, that was Eliot at his best, ever dealing in the concrete and inimitable and thus memorable images in his early poems and great tragedies. In this respect, Eliot started out with a bang, "not a whimper," in his first published poem, "The Love Song of J. Alfred Prufrock," with its treasury of innovative phrases, all of them gold doubloons in refreshing uniqueness.

But we shall not dwell upon the incomparable imagery that startled the poetic world in Harriet Monroe's *Poetry* magazine. Instead, we are concerned with the Christian tragic hero, whom Eliot (perhaps describing himself, as he visualized himself to be in time and space in time to come) describes thusly:

> *No, I am not Prince Hamlet, nor was meant to be;*
> *Am an attendant lord, one that will do*
> *To swell a progress, start a scene or two,*
> *Advise the prince; no doubt, an easy tool,*
> *Deferential, glad to be of use,*
> *Politic, cautious, and meticulous;*
> *Full of high sentence, but a bit obtuse;*
> *At times, indeed, almost ridiculous—*
> *Almost, at times, the Fool.*

This is the essential Prufrock of the singular, acerbic poem. This is Eliot, too, then and there and in time to come, as he thought then and there. Probably, he had despaired of Conrad Aiken's ever placing the poem, though Ezra Pound later placed it for him after much effort, blood, sweat, tears, and toil. To be sure, the Christian elements of the poem are not explicit, or spelled out; but they are nonetheless implicit, or emphatically hinted at. We refer especially to the Christian (and also Anglo-Catholic) concept of existential despair at never actualizing the ideal; or, as Eliot summarizes the sense of existential nausea for the Catholic:

> *We have lingered in the chambers of the sea*
> *By sea-girls wreathed in the seaweed red and brown*
> *Till human voices wake us, and we drown.*

Is evolution at work, or a hint of hope for the meaningful existential option, in itself the definition of Christian free will? In "Portrait of a Lady," Eliot's metaphorical and metaphysical lips fairly curl as he terminates the poem:

> *Well and what if she should die some afternoon,*

Afternoon grey and smoky, evening yellow and rose;
Should die and leave me sitting pen in hand
With the smoke coming down above the housetops;
Doubtful, for a while,
Not knowing what to feel or if I understand
Or whether wise or foolish, tardy or too soon . . .
Would she not have the advantage, after all?
This music is successful with a "dying fall"
Now that we talk of dying—
And should I have the right to smile?

Perhaps this last time, in Eliot's mind (for he was ever something of a dour Calvinist and not the Anglo-Catholic he presumed himself to be), that even man, wretched man, was not totally damned: had life: enjoyed life: thus had rights: could aspire to a meaningful option: thus would aspire to personal happiness: even, in time to come, aspire to Christian salvation.

Yet the mood is unequal, for the conviction is unsteady. In "Preludes," a short poem, yet one of Eliot's imagistically most successful poems, he concludes, as we infer:

Wipe your hand across your mouth, and laugh;
The worlds revolve like ancient women
Gathering fuel in vacant lots.

So, in a word, Eliot, at this point of his evolution (with his ever-pronounced Puritanism, in evolution to Jansenism), does not even dare to dare to hope to hope.

The following poems are equally memorable: "Rhapsody on a Windy Night," with its concluding line, "The last twist of the knife," which twists in our faithless heart. In "Mr. Apollinax," he concludes with biting sarcasm and pithy poignancy: "Of dowager Mrs. Phlaccus, and Professor and Mrs. Cheetah/ I remember a slice of lemon, and a bitter macaroon." The following poems are also memorable: "Conversation Galante," with "Are we then so serious?"; and "La Figlia che Piange," with "Sometimes these cogitations still amaze/ The troubled midnight and the noon's repose." It is existential despair that Eliot describes, as he says in "Gerontion," one of his strongest poems:

I that was near your heart was removed therefrom
To lose beauty in terror, terror in inquisition.
I have lost my passion: why should I need to keep it

> *Since what is kept must be adulterated?*
> *I have lost my sight, smell, hearing, taste and touch:*
> *How should I use them for your closer contact?*

"Contact" is the key word in the poem, for it depicts the prevailing leitmotif of the love motif of the Christian communist *koinonia,* or community. Of course, Eliot is not yet a professed Anglo-Catholic, but he is definitely moving toward Catholicism: toward "contact": and thus toward Christian "commitment": in a kind of existential "engagement": in *"koinonia":* with the meaningful and healing existential option of Christian love.

There are other great poems among Eliot's early work with the same themes, the identical concerns. In "Burbank with a Baedeker: Bleistein with a Cigar," we see the memorable lines:

> *But this or such was Bleistein's way:*
> *A saggy bending of the knees*
> *And elbows, with the palms turned out,*
> *Chicago Semite Viennese.*

Nowhere is the contemporary antihero more clearly evidenced than in "Sweeney Erect," where Eliot cogently observes:

> *(The lengthened shadow of a man*
> *Is history, said Emerson*
> *Who had not seen the silhouette*
> *Of Sweeney straddled in the sun.)*

In "Sweeney among the Nightingales," Eliot depicts decadent spleen, which paralyzes Christian free will in abulia and obviates existential option:

> *She and the lady in the cape*
> *Are suspect, thought to be in league;*
> *Therefore the man with heavy eyes*
> *Declines the gambit, shows fatigue.*

Clearly, Eliot already approaches Christian considerations of the human condition, as he explicitly formulates in "The Hippopotamus," or the Catholic Church mired in "humanity" (existential thinginess), which also paralyzes free will. Concluding hopefully (but the tone, at this point in his spiritual development, is forced), he writes meaningfully, also apocalyptically:

> *He shall be washed as white as snow,*
> *By all the martyr'd virgins kist,*
> *While the True Church remains below*
> *Wrapt in the old miasmal mist.*

Thus, in his first great efforts, Eliot expresses himself at the height of his creative power: in a kind of Carlylean "Everlasting No," yes: but also, in this poem, foreshadowing his professed and genuine Catholic Christianity (which was heavily Puritan, or, at least, Jansenist) in a Carlylean "Everlasting Yea."

After considering Eliot's early masterpieces, we are now ready to mention his first great failure, the noblest failure of the English language, and though a failure, yet the greatest poem of the twentieth century, which, along with Ernest Hemingway's *The Sun Also Rises,* was known as the philosophy of the Lost Generation: despair: disillusionment. From our standpoint, the reason for the artistic failure of "The Waste Land" is readily and painfully apparent. In the words of Edgar Allan Poe, the father of French symbolism and that currently much underrated giant of American literature, the successful work of art must create a central impression; that is precisely what Eliot's "The Waste Land" does not do, and that is why we now point out its obvious limitation despite the lavish encomia it has so unjustly received. In a word, who are the personae, or speakers? The Fisher King of the Grail legends? "The Hanged Man" of the Tarot cards? The drowned Phoenician sailor, Phlebus? Ferdinand, Prince of Naples, from Shakespeare's *The Tempest,* itself a poor romance? Christ (and he seems very pagan in this study in comparative religion)? Tristan? Parsifal? St. Augustine? Several Biblical prophets, all of them unkempt and rather dirty? Tiresias, the blind seer of Homer's *Odyssey?* Euripides' *Bacchae* and *Phoenissae?* Sophocles' Theban plays? The three Thames daughters patterned after the Rhine maidens of Wagner's *Ring of the Nibelungen* tetralogy? There are simply too many speakers with too many strident voices and with too much dissonance and discordance to give Edgar Allan Poe's central idea: central impression. Yes, we admit that there are many memorable lines, and we argue that these are why the poem is really remembered (somewhat unjustly), rather than for the central impression. The strength and weakness of "The Waste Land" are readily seen from the section "The Fire Sermon," ostensibly taken from Buddha's sermon of that name against the futility and absurdity of carnal love:

> *She turns and looks a moment in the glass,*
> *Hardly aware of her departed lover;*
> *Her brain allows one half-formed thought to pass:*

> *"Well now that's done: and I'm glad it's over."*
> *When lovely woman stoops to folly and*
> *Paces about her room again, alone,*
> *She smoothes her hair with automatic hand,*
> *And puts a record on the gramophone.*

This, indeed, is heady poetry: gamey: most successful (forceful) within its constricted limit. But it really isn't great literature, is it? Is it really the equivalent of Buddha's impassioned diatribe against the metaphysical absurdity of desire? In summary, for these examples could be multiplied *ad infinitum* and *nauseam,* the notes really hold our interest more than the poem itself, though Eliot himself decried their original inclusion for the necessity of the signature. At least, these notes indicate the remarkable order within Eliot's mind at the religiously critical time of the composition of "The Waste Land." The poem itself, most regrettably, is too chaotic to achieve the stature of traditionally conceived great art, which should always present an overwhelming central impression. In "The Waste Land," the central idea is simply that of existential despair, nausea, disillusionment; and while this was sufficient to attract the attention of Gertrude Stein's readers *entre les deux guerres,* we doubt that it contains the positive substance for permanent inclusion in the canon of great English literature.

In "The Hollow Men," however, Eliot returns to his established greatness; and this is imagistically and philosophically one of the major poems of English literature. There are many memorable lines, all contributing to the integrity of the aesthetic whole (central impression); but these verses most readily remain in the memory:

> *This is the dead land*
> *This is cactus land*
> *Here the stone images*
> *Are raised, here they receive*
> *The supplication of a dead man's hand*
> *Under the twinkle of a fading star.*

Too, the poem does not "end with a whimper" but rather with the calculated effect of a verbal bang: literary impact. It is one of the glories of English literature, all the more so as it depicts the certain failure of good men with great aspirations, Kurtz and Guy Fawkes, who simply could not deliver the metaphysical goods (so to speak) with their existential options.

Then, in 1930, Eliot remains in the grand manner with "Ash-Wednesday," now the assured and assurable expression of his Anglo-Catholicism—or, as we prefer to think of it, English Catholicism. In the poem, there are more memorable lines, certainly, but none more meaningful than these, which cut to the bone and marrow—and heart:

> *This is the time of tension between dying and birth*
> *The place of solitude where three dreams cross*
> *Between blue rocks*
> *But when the voices shaken from the yew-tree drift away*
> *Let the other yew be shaken and reply . . . .*
>
> *And let my cry come unto Thee.*

Certainly, it is the impassioned cry of the Christian sinner in existential despair. Too, it has parallels in the penitent's submission in Islam, if not Calvinism. Moreover, it has instructive parallels in other languages and literatures and religions. In a sense, too, it represents a Calvinist notion of predestination and the doctrine of the elect; for although it has not been sufficiently pointed out, Eliot, born and reared a strange kind of Unitarian, was really as Calvinist as Catholic. However this may be to his philosophical confusion, the cry of the Christian tragic hero is authentic. It comes both from the heart and the syrupy entrails, and it has an admirable artistic integrity: because it creates an overwhelming central impression and thus has an undeniable and ineffable artistic impact upon us.

Shortly thereafter, we find Eliot's artistically perfect poem, "Journey of the Magi," a minor masterpiece of the English language, though "The Love Song of J. Alfred Prufrock" and "The Hollow Men" and "Gerontion" have greater depth, dimension, impact, sheer and even brute force. From the standpoint of the Christian tragic hero, "Journey of the Magi" tells how each believer dies in and for and through Christ, and him crucified, the Redeemer, all Christians redeeming themselves (too) through their vicarious participation in Christ's death:

> *All this was a long time ago, I remember,*
> *And I would do it again, but set down*
> *This set down*
> *This: were we led all that way for*
> *Birth or Death? There was a Birth, certainly,*
> *We had evidence and no doubt. I had seen birth and death,*
> *But had thought they were different; this Birth was*

> *Hard and bitter agony for us, like Death, our death.*
> *We returned to our places, these Kingdoms,*
> *But no longer at ease here, in the old dispensation,*
> *With an alien people clutching their gods.*
> *I should be glad of another death.*

While these lines depict the Christian tragic hero, they are imagistically the least satisfactory of the poem; they point with absolute certainty to the kind of writing that results in the aesthetic failure of "The Four Quartets," which after "The Waste Land" may be the noblest failure in English literature.

"A Song for Simeon," "Animula," and "Marina" also show Eliot in aesthetic and religious transition and evolution, yet at the height of his remarkable imagistic powers (for which almost alone, one day, we shall remember him) in certain notable verses, though at the same time wondrously diffuse (and perhaps a bit obtuse, too?) in certain other verses. For example, "Animula" is truly a remarkable poem, as we admit. But could one really visualize a more ineffective, anticlimactic, and prosaic dénouement—or "catastrophe," in the Greek sense of "rounding off"?

> *Pray for Guiterriez, avid of speed and power,*
> *For Boudin, blown to pieces,*
> *For this one who made a great fortune,*
> *And that one who went his own way.*
> *Pray for Floret, by the boarhound slain between the yew trees,*
> *Pray for us now and at the hour of our birth.*

Moreover, and likewise, the conclusion of "Marina," while memorable and most imagistic, is quite diffuse and inexact:

> *What seas what shores what granite islands*
> *And woodthrush calling through the fog*
> *My daughter.*

From this time on, apparently, Eliot is in an aesthetic decline, while his Christian connections seem to increase. "Sweeney Agonistes," for example, has highly satisfactory lines; but it does not present an aesthetic whole and, in this sense, lacks artistic integrity. So, too, it is with "Coriolan," "Difficulties of a Statesman," and all the minor poems, including especially the nonsensical poems from "Old Possum's Book of Practical Cats," itself only Lewis Carroll at his cutesy best. But perhaps the dying swan always utters a last message, and Eliot has never surpassed himself in certain of the lines from "Choruses from The Rock":

> *The desert is not remote in southern tropics,*
> *The desert is not only around the corner,*
> *The desert is squeezed in the tube-train next to you,*
> *The desert is in the heart of your brother.*

These lines are strong and memorable, yes, but they are more philosophy than poetry, and from this point on, Eliot degenerates in his verse to the positive nadir (and sometimes poetic blather) of "The Four Quartets."

Perhaps, indeed, we are edified by inspirational sermons from a good Catholic pulpit. But are they ever really literature? Is even Bossuet, in his *Oraisons funèbres,* really great literature? For that matter, if we are honest, are even some Bible passages effective storytelling, as Oscar Wilde has rightly (though perhaps sacrilegiously) questioned?

Now we are ready to consider "The Four Quartets": "Burnt Norton," "East Coker," "The Dry Salvages," and "Little Gidding." The total effect disappoints us because these four poems do not really represent distinct *personae,* or poetic narrators. An analogy may be instructive, especially since "The Four Quartets" approximate the role and function of the chorus in Greek tragedy.

Of course, we admit that the chorus serves an invaluable function in Greek tragedy; and some of the poetry takes one's aesthetic breath away, which is true of "The Four Quartets," too. But what is important in Greek tragedy are the protagonists, while the chorus merely reflects upon the actions and attitudes of the protagonists. The protagonists represent *kinesis,* while the chorus represents *stasis.* Likewise, in Eliot's imaginative work, the *personae* represent *kinesis,* or dynamic development, while "The Four Quartets" represents *stasis,* or pietistic (and very Catholic, or really Jansenist) reflection upon four geographical locations, visited by imaginary interlocutors concerned with *koinonia* and consumed by *caritas.*

Once again, we respectively dissent from the whole body of Eliot criticism, which regards "The Four Quartets" as the crowning achievement of the poet's life. We believe that Eliot is at his best, as in these lines from "Burnt Norton," only when he is imagistically concrete:

> *Time and the bell have buried the day.*
> *The black cloud carries the sun away.*
> *Will the sunflower turn to us, will the clematis*

> *Stray down, bend to us; tendril and spray*
> *Clutch and cling?*
> *Chill*
> *Fingers of yew be curled*
> *Down on us? After the kingfisher's wing*
> *Has answered to light, and is silent, the light is still*
> *At the still point of the turning world.*

These lines represent something of the early Eliot, though they are far more pietistic, perhaps to the detriment of impact.

From "East Coker" we have chosen a passage to evidence our point about the parallel of "The Four Quartets" with the Greek chorus from classical tragedy:

> *O dark dark dark. They all go into the dark,*
> *The vacant interstellar places, the vacant into the vacant,*
> *The captains, merchant bankers, eminent men of letters,*
> *The generous patrons of arts, the statesmen and the rulers,*
> *Distinguished civil servants, chairmen of many committees,*
> *Industrial lords and petty contractors, all go into the dark,*
> *And dark the sun and moon, and the Almanach de Gotha*
> *And the Stock Exchange Gazette, the Directory of Directors,*
> *And cold the sense and lost the motive of action.*
> *And we all go with them, into the silent funeral,*
> *Nobody's funeral, for there is no one to bury.*
> *I said to my soul, be still, and let the dark come upon you*
> *Which shall be the darkness of God.*

This is good poetry, but is also *static* poetry. It represents the pietistic reflection of a Catholic breviary or of the Anglican *Book of Common Prayer.* In our aesthetic theory, it is simply not *dynamic* enough to be the kind of immortal literature that most critics have claimed it is. It does not portray the *kinesis* of man's soul in search of God, but rather a *static* reflection upon that singular search and perhaps not even on God (as Object) so much as on the thrill of the sacred quest itself.

In "The Dry Salvages," once again, we hear the mournful *static* cry of the Greek chorus:

> *Where is there an end of it, the soundless wailing,*
> *The silent withering of autumn flowers*

Dripping their petals and remaining motionless;
Where is there an end to the drifting wreckage,
The prayer of the bone on the beach, the unprayable
Prayer at the calamitous annunciation?

We know of no better examples of *stasis* except in the poems of Leconte de Lisle (repeatedly, "tout se tait"), himself a pagan, while Eliot is a devout and even pietistic Catholic. But while these lines satisfy our religious sense as fellow Catholics, they do not really stir us aesthetically, imagistically, psychologically, even philosophically, as do "Prufrock," "Gerontion," "The Hollow Men," or, in a lesser vein, "Journey of the Magi." Pietism may very well get a proper penitent duly into Purgatory and ultimately into Paradise, but it does not mean that the poet is a great writer. For *stasis* in literature, by definition, cannot be so dramatic (and thus take our aesthetic breath away in certain impact) as *kinesis* can.

At least, despite this noble failure of "The Four Quartets," Eliot is most at home in "Little Gidding," for that Catholic community appealed to Eliot, particularly since it was destroyed by his archenemies, Cromwell's Puritans as *anti-catholiques farouches*. As in most of Eliot, he starts off with a verbal bang, though he lamentably ends "Little Gidding" with a subdued whimper:

Midwinter spring is its own season
Sempiternal though sodden towards sundown,
Suspended in time, between pole and tropic.
When the short day is brightest, with frost and fire,
The brief sun flames the ice, on pond and ditches,
In windless cold that is the heart's heat,
Reflecting in a watery mirror
A glare that is blindness in the early afternoon.
And glow more intense than blaze of branch, or brazier,
Stirs the dumb spirit: no wind, but pentecostal fire
In the dark time of the year. Between melting and freezing
The soul's sap quivers. There is no earth smell
Or smell of living thing. This is the spring time
But not in time's covenant. Now the hedgerow
Is blanched for an hour with transitory blossom
Of snow, a bloom more sudden
Than that of summer, neither budding nor fading,
Not in the scheme of generation,

> *Where is the summer, the unimaginable*
> *Zero summer?*

While these lines are certainly beautiful and most memorable, they are also static, and thus they lack dramatic direction as well as progression: movement toward a central impression, governed by a central idea. For this reason, we insist that "Little Gidding," like the other three quartets, lacks the impact (the verbal and metaphysical slap in the face) that Eliot ever gives us in his early poems. Regrettably, "The Four Quartets" remains a noble failure, after "The Waste Land," the noblest failure in the English language. For what sophisticated reader can lose himself in the honied and sometimes cloying diction of a Catholic breviary?

To our mind, it is significant that Eliot wrote no more serious poetry after "The Four Quartets." Nearly all critics say that he had reached the pinnacle of his poetic powers, that he gave up on poetry because he could go no higher, no farther, just as Dante could go no higher than the Light Scene in the concluding canto of "Paradise." But Dante was at his best in "Inferno," and Eliot was at his best in the early poems of despair and disillusionment. His powers were at their height in "Journey of the Magi," which yet showed a certain decline, decay, even *faisandage,* since the poem doesn't slap us in the face. We really believe that by the time he wrote "The Four Quartets," Eliot realized his poetic powers were in such demonstrable decline and fall that he turned his diminishing energies to the drama, instead, in aesthetic appreciation of this fact. To return to our favorite metaphor, great art always has the impact of a slap on the face. Eliot, by now, was absorbed in the Catholic breviary, like the bewitchingly beautiful *Book of Kells,* which, though beautiful, did not have the overwhelming impact of Dante's "Inferno," just as all great art knocks down, floors, perhaps knocks out, the sensitive reader.

By now, Eliot had already interested himself in the pageant play "The Rock" (1934) and in the tragic Christian drama *Murder in the Cathedral* (1935, at Canterbury). "The Rock" is extremely powerful, though the stasis of the chorus makes it evident to us that Eliot has begun his visible decline of poetic powers. A year later, in *Murder in the Cathedral,* Eliot admirably combines stasis and kinesis. The protagonist, or Christian tragic hero, is Thomas à Beckett, Archbishop of Canterbury, a Christ-figure, who has an irreconcilable conflict with the English king. It is the closest play to Greek tragedy that we have in English drama: starkly beautiful, strangely compelling, an admirable elixir of *stasis* (chorus) and *kinesis* (the dynamic changes in ecclesiastical response to "Caesar").

Obviously, once again, Eliot is concerned with *koinonia* and *caritas*. Beckett explains why, as a sensualist reformed, he, now a living saint, also soon a Christian tragic hero, must oppose the king, once his friend and fellow debauchee, and his friend because of a common debauchery:

> *Temporal power, to build a good world,*
> *To keep order, as the world knows order,*
> *Those who put their faith in worldly order*
> *Not controlled by the order of God,*
> *In confident ignorance, but arrest disorder,*
> *Make it fast, breed fatal disease,*
> *Degrade what they exalt, Power with the King—*
> *I was the king, his arm, his better reason.*
> *But what was once exaltation*
> *Would now be only mean descent.*

Is Christ or, in this case, Beckett, the Christian tragic hero, not always opposed to Caesar, now the English king? Yet it is part of the tragedy, as the knights cogently argue, that Thomas seeks his own martyrdom in a kind of physical and spiritual suicide. The knights have a valid point to make, which the Christian critics usually gloss over. Thomas himself, however, is acutely aware of this *hamartia* within himself, the consciously effective will to martyrdom in a service of God that is also selfishly a service of egotistic self:

> *Now is my way clear, now is the meaning plain:*
> *Temptation shall not come in this kind again.*
> *The last temptation is the greatest treason:*
> *To do the right deed for the wrong reason.*

Never did Eliot surpass himself in this cogent analysis of the Christian tragic hero, who, in the end, was not a martyr for the sake of martyrdom, but rather to claim the sanctity of his *koinonia* in and through his *caritas,* itself a self-less love for the selfless (and truly communist) Christian "community," i.e., the Church Militant.

In *The Family Reunion* (1939), Eliot, drawing upon the Eumenides, which he mistranslates as the Furies (actually the Erinyes, while the Eumenides are the "Gracious Ones" of atonement and forgiveness), re-creates a modern Greek tragedy in the highly poetic terms of a family curse. Stated baldly, Harry Lord Monchensey, at historic Wishwood, thinks he murdered his wife at sea and that the Furies have pursued him ever since. The family, however, is convinced that he is suffering delusions of guilt. To some extent, Eliot's play is based on Aeschylus' *Oresteia* trilogy (*Agamemnon, The Choëphoroe, The Eumenides*). Probably, he did not commit the murder, though psychologically he willed it—and thus perhaps, in a metaphysical sense, called her death into being. What, indeed, is the act of murder anyway?

> *It is really harder to believe in murder*
> *Than to believe in cancer. Cancer is here:*
> *The lump, the dull pain, the occasional sickness:*
> *Murder a reversal of sleep and waking.*
> *Murder was there. Your ordinary murderer*
> *Regards himself as an innocent victim.*
> *To himself he is still what used to be*
> *Or what he would be. He cannot realize*
> *That everything is irrevocable,*
> *The part unredeemable.*

What is redemption, indeed, but the commitment of self through *caritas* to actualizing the ideal of *koinonia?* Nowhere did Eliot state this tenet more clearly than in *The Family Reunion,* surely the contemporary setting to the more austere, more successful, but not more Catholic *Murder in the Cathedral.*

In 1949, Eliot drops to the nadir of his poetic and philosophical powers in *The Cocktail Party,* itself highly successful on the commercial stage. It isn't that the design isn't worthwhile, for it is: as the presentation of seven souls, each capable of a different level of saintliness, so that the calendar saint (as with Thomas a Beckett) is grandly—and perhaps a trifle grandiosely, too— no longer such a consuming concern. The least satisfactory aspect of the play is its set of stereotypes—Lavinia and Edward, the oh-so-sophisticated couple of the casual adultery, and especially, too, and even more so, Sir Henry Harcourt-Reilly, a psychiatrist who turns out to be the Unidentified Guest of Act One. His appearance, in a word, is the kernel of the problem, since he may actually represent God in omniscience. For really, most psychiatry is (as it is here) at philosophical odds with Christian self-actualization, and it is difficult to see how the Anglo-Saxons and Germans fell for it, while the Latins never did. The psychiatrists' explanation of man is not that of the religious *vates,* even in the case of C. G. Jung, whom Eliot knew only secondhand and didn't sufficiently appreciate anyway. Reilly's analysis of the human condition, for example, is surprisingly one-dimensional, as it takes man's glands and muscles and viscera into consideration, but not very much his psyche:

> *Maintain themselves by the common routine,*
> *Learn to avoid successive expectation,*
> *Become tolerant of themselves and others,*
> *Giving and taking, in the usual actions*
> *What there is to give and take. They do not repine;*
> *Are contented with the morning that separates*
> *And with the evening that brings together*
> *For casual talk before the fire*
> *Two people who know they do not understand each other,*
> *Breeding children whom they do not understand*
> *And who will never understand them.*

This psychiatric gibberish, a veritable geyser of pish-posh, does not represent Dante at all or Baudelaire at his best. Emphatically, too, it does Eliot no real service in his keen and cutting formulation of the spiritual *Angst* of the Christian tragic hero. By all means, God is no mere modern psychiatrist, into the insidious subleties of a double-bind depth therapy of the Palo Alto school of Bateson.

Eliot's *The Confidential Clerk,* or "private secretary" (1954), is very much like an overplotted Roman comedy; and that, in essence, is its most glaring fault. Moreover, it borders on the grotesque, not merely the Lewis Carroll whimsicalities of "Old Possum's Book of Practical Cats," but really into the baroque and the grotesque. For example, the totally absurd plot reads that Sir Claude and Lady Elizabeth Mulhammer each had a baby born of wedlock a quarter-century before. Or, rephrased, Sir Claude thought he had, though in reality the pregnant woman died before giving birth. The baby, Colby, he thought was his was really the son of her widowed and destitute sister, Mrs. Guzzard. Lady Elizabeth's child had been placed with a nurse by her fiancé; and when a rhinoceros killed the child in Africa (*sic,* incredibly enough), the family denied all responsibility for the child, and Elizabeth was unable to locate her baby.

So it is an absurd plot, even truly grotesque, luxuriously Roman, as if out of Plautus and Terence, not at all starkly Greek out of Aeschylus and Sophocles. Clearly, Eliot is at the end of his poetic inspiration and his religious sensibilities. He is merely repeating himself, almost vainly, with the *porte-paroles* of other characters in other plays, mouthing the same "cute" modern philosophy that is too one-dimensional for Catholicism in its maturity. Interestingly enough, nobody seems to speak in particular for the poet, Eliot himself. For this, at least, we are grateful; it only proves our thesis that Eliot was by now consciously aware that his creative inspiration had been exhausted.

In *The Elder Statesman,* Eliot is at the very nadir of his powers, as he takes for his model *Oedipus at Colonus,* the anticlimax of Sophocles in his spectacular literary career. But what is important for us in this play, despite its singular lack of imagistic impact, is the author's insistence on love, *caritas.* Of course, Sophocles' play is not fully integrated in *The Elder Statesman,* but Oedipus' love for his children also depicts Lord Claverton's concern and spiritual care for his children. It is a mature play for a mature audience; Lord Claverton is the Christian tragic hero as a father who certainly cares, who emphatically loves, but who had failed. At least, love can exert a healing power: This is Eliot's message in a play that is too attenuated to achieve impact and is thus a dramatic failure.

What, in summary, are our impressions of T. S. Eliot as his own Christian tragic hero, glimpsed only partially and always incompletely in the *personae* of his various poems and plays? Still, what is the general impression, despite our startling claim that Eliot's aesthetic powers declined and did not ascend until the day when, as in the failure of *The Elder Statesman,* he went out truly, not with a bang but a whimper? For, in sober truth, Eliot most succeeds artistically in his great poems of despair and disillusionment before he formally embraces Anglo-Catholicism as properly the English expression of two thousand years of Catholic Christianity.

We have noted that Eliot, throughout his work—gloriously implicit in the early poems, explicit often as noble failures in the later poems and plays—is concerned with the Christian tragic hero in the context of *caritas* and *koinonia.* In other words, what is the Christian's relationship to self, society, and God? In this respect, we feel that Eliot, who was probably the most erudite man who ever wrote in English, and who may have been our greatest poet after Shakespeare, really didn't like himself very much for his very human failings as an animal: He simply couldn't accept his baser self, his carnal nature, his Dionysian tendencies, which all animals have. Consequently, he is ill at ease in the *koinonia* with his fellow Christians, like Paul Claudel, who, though devout, had a true carnal nature, like most Catholic Christians. Eliot is the poet of eternal Lent, while Catholics also need Mardi Gras and carnival, which Eliot could never accept. Since Eliot lacks all joy and never expresses the least modicum of joy, Christian or carnal, in his work, his *koinonia* is drear, drab, ever cold, always cheerless.

In fact, Eliot is not really a Catholic in the broadest sense of the word, though he prided himself on his connection with Dante (who emphatically expresses spiritual joy) and with Baudelaire (who emphatically expresses Dionysian or carnal joy). Eliot is really a Jansenist, a pietist, who had made for himself an elaborate dungeon at an ornate and elaborate Port-Royal of the spirit, in which he walks alone through formal gardens, his Catholic breviary in hand, afraid of a baser (thus more catholic) self he can never accept, his eyes ever on pietist literature (like the noble failure of "The Four Quartets"), noble failures all of man's highest aspirations for the unattainable divine, since man is not divine. And as he walks in quiet despair and even quieter desperation, he dares not lift his eyes to heaven to confront a dour, Calvinist God who is truly too Puritanical, too harsh, too unforgiving, and far too cold, to be the historic Catholic God of *caritas* and *koinonia*, which Eliot so tragically professes in his religious failure to distinguish between his Catholic vision of truth and the professed reality of truth professed by the Catholic churches to which, alas, he gives only lip service.

Bibliography of References

Abraham, Claude. *Jean Racine*. Boston: Twayne, 1977.

Bishop, Morris. *Pascal, the Life of Genius*. New York: Reynal and Hitchcock, 1936.

Bradley, A.C. *Shakespearean Tragedy*. New York: Macmillan, 1967.

Brengle, Richard L. *Arthur, King of Britain: History, Romance, Chronicle and Criticism*. New York: Appleton-Century-Crofts, 1964.

Bruce, James Douglas. *The Evolution of Arthurian Romance from the Beginnings Down to the Year 1300*. Baltimore: Johns Hopkins Press, 1923.

Butler, Philip. *Classicisme et baroque dans l'oeuvre de Racine*. Paris: Nizet, 1959.

Cailliet, Emile. *Pascal: The Emergence of Genius*. New York: Greenwood Press, 1967.

Campbell, Lily B. *Shakespeare's Tragic Heroes: Slaves of Passion*. Cambridge: Cambridge University Press, 1930.

Cazamian, L. *A History of French Literature*. Oxford: Clarendon Press, 1955.

Chaigne, Louis. *Paul Claudel: The Man and the Mystic*. New York: Appleton-Century-Crofts, 1961.

Chute, Marchette. *Geoffrey Chaucer of England*. New York: Dutton, 1946.

Duggan, Joseph J. *The Song of Roland: Formulaic Style and Poetic Craft*. Berkeley: University of California Press, 1973.

Ellis-Fermor, Una. *Shakespeare the Dramatist and Other Papers*. New York: Barnes and Noble, 1961.

Emerson, Ralph Waldo. "Montaigne or the Skeptic," from *Represenstative Men: Seven Lectures*. Boston: Phillips and Sampson, 1850.

Fox, John. *A Literary History of France: The Middle Ages*. New York: Barnes and Noble, 1974.

Frame, Donald M. *Montaigne's Discovery of Man: The Humanization of the Humanist*. New York: Columbia University Press, 1955.

_____. *Montaigne: A Biography*. New York: Harcourt, Brace, and World, 1965.

_____. *Complete Works.* Stanford: Stanford University Press, 1958.

Frazer, Sir James George. *The Golden Bough.* New York: St. Martin's Press, 1976.

Frye, Northrop. *Fearful Symmetry.* Princeton: Princeton University Press, 1947.

Frye, Roland Mushat. *Shakespeare and Christian Doctrine.* Princeton: Princeton University Press, 1963.

Gleckner, Robert F. *The Piper and the Bard.* Detroit: Wayne State University Press, 1959.

Holzknecht, Karl J. *The Backgrounds of Shakespeare's Plays.* New York: American Book Company, 1950.

Hubert, Immanuel. *The Critique of Pure Reason.* New York: Modern Library, 1958.

Lawrence, William Witherle. *Chaucer and the Canterbury Tales.* New York: Biblo and Tannen, 1969.

Loomis, Roger Sherman. *Arthurian Tradition and Chrétien de Troyes.* New York: Columbia University Press, 1949.

Malone, Kemp. *Chapters on Chaucer.* Baltimore: Johns Hopkins Press, 1968.

Micha, Alexandre. *Le Singulier Montaigne.* Paris: Nizet, 1964.

Miel, Jan. *Pascal and Theology.* Baltimore: Johns Hopkins Press, 1969.

Moreau, Pierre. *Montaigne: l'Homme et l'Oeuvre.* Paris: Boivin, 1939.

Mornet, Daniel. *Jean Racine.* Paris: Aux Armes de France, 1944.

Mossop, D.J. *Baudelaire's Tragic Hero: A Study of the Architecture of "Les Fleurs du mal."* London: Oxford University Press, 1961.

Owen, Douglas David Roy. *The Evolution of the Grail Legend.* Edinburgh: University of St. Andrew's, 1968.

Pater, Walter. *The Renaissance.* New York: Boni and Liveright, 1919.

Plattard, Jean. *Montaigne et son temps.* Paris: Boivin, 1933.

Rhys, John. *Studies in the Arthurian Legend.* New York: Russell and Russell, 1966.

Robertson, D.W., Jr. *A Preface to Chaucer: Studies in Medieval Perspectives.* Princeton: Princeton University Press, 1962.

Robinson, F.N. *The Works of Geoffrey Chaucer.* Boston: Houghton Mifflin, 1957.

Rowse, A.L. *William Shakespeare.* New York: Harper and Row, 1963.

Tillyard, E.M.W. *Milton.* London: Chatto and Windus, 1967.

_____. *Studies in Milton.* London: Chatto and Windus, 1951.

Wagenknecht, Edward. *Chaucer: Essays in Criticism.* New York: Oxford University Press, 1959.

_____. *The Personality of Milton.* Norman: University of Oklahoma Press, 1970.

Weston, Jesse L. *From Ritual to Romance.* Garden City, New York: Doubleday, 1957.

Wilson, Mona. *The Life of William Blake.* New York: Cooper Square Publishers, 1969.

INDEX: The Christian Tragic Hero